"This saga takes the reader into many amusing, scary and exciting situations. It is very rich reading for all of us who always wanted to cruise, but didn't. When the episode is concluded, you find yourself wishing for more."
Edwin P. Brown, President
Maritime Heritage Alliance

"A great sailing adventure! Exciting and easy to read; arouses curiosity as to what will happen next. Certainly a must reading for boaters and adventuresome people of all walks of life."
Orval and Mary Center, Retired
District Manager, NCR

"How exciting to read how the author enjoyed and coped when she was faced with the challenges of living aboard a sailboat for two years."
Betty Lou Savage, Retired Registered Nurse

"I felt as if I had just finished a two year cruise, was with them and saw all the sights."
Eunice Isaac

"This book is very, very interesting. Suspense holds the readers' attention. It makes for continuous reading without stopping."
William and Marian Ragsdale, Retired
District Manager, Amoco Oil (Ind.)

"Very interesting and informative for both the armchair sailor and those who plan to live aboard. Excellent also for anyone who enjoys traveling. One can learn from others' experiences."
John R. Dost, Boat Builder
Schooner *Madeline*

To my husband
Kenneth R. Hoekwater,
captain of PRIME TIME

MY HOME AFLOAT

Taken from My Journal of a Two Year Voyage aboard

PRIME TIME

DOROTHY I. HOEKWATER

Prime Time Publishing
Fort Myers, Florida

MY HOME AFLOAT

Taken from my Journal of a Two Year Voyage aboard

PRIME TIME

By Dorothy I. Hoekwater

Published by:
> Prime Time Publishing
> 5688 Balkan Court, SW
> Fort Myers, Florida 33919

First printing 1992

Printed in the United States of America

Library of Congress Catalog Number 92–093407

ISBN 0–9632888–4–9

*Additional copies of this book may be ordered
through bookstores or by sending
$9.95 plus $3.50
for postage and handling to:*
Publishers Distribution Service
6893 Sullivan Road
Grawn, Michigan 49637
or
by VISA or Master Charge by calling:
(800) 345-0096

Publisher's Cataloging-in-Publication Data

Hoekwater, Dorothy I.
    My home afloat: taken from my journal of a two year voyage aboard Prime Time / Dorothy I. Hoekwater. -- Fort Myers, Fla.: Prime Time Pub.,
       p. cm. photos
       Includes index
       ISBN: 0-9632888-4-9

       1. Hoekwater, Dorothy I. 2. Prime Time (Sailboat) 3. Mississippi River-Description and travel. 4. Gulf Intracoastal Waterway-Description and travel. 5. Atlantic Coast (U.S.)-Description and travel. 6. Bahamas--Description and travel--1982-1984 I. Title.

E169.04H64
917.3'0927 dc20   92-123456

Manufactured in the United States of America

TABLE OF CONTENTS

PAGE

11   1   "WE'RE GOING TO DO WHAT?"
          "SELL THE HOUSE AND LIVE ON THE BOAT"
15   2   Traverse City–Chicago
21   3   Chicago–Mississippi River
27   4   Introduction to Mississippi River

37   5   Lower Mississippi River
51   6   Memphis–New Orleans
61   7   It Was a Great Experience–But
65   8   The Intercoastal Waterway (ICW)

69   9   Big Day/Night Across the Gulf
73   10   Tarpon Springs–Fort Myers
77   11   "Winter" at Fort Myers
81   12   Fort Myers–Key West

87   13   Dry Tortugas
91   14   Key West–Miami–Heading North
95   15   Miami–Norfolk
103   16   Norfolk–Cape May–New Jersey

107   17   Cape May–New York
109   18   New York–Maine
119   19   Maine
123   20   Mount Katahdin, Baxter State Park

131	21	Trying to Get Back to the Boat
135	22	Return Trip South -Cape Cod Canal
139	23	Buzzards Bay-Hell Gate
143	24	Hell Gate-Cape May
145	25	Cape May-Norfolk
149	26	Back on Waterway
151	27	Going Home
153	28	Back on Waterway-Marathon
157	29	Marathon-Fort Myers
159	30	Fort Myers-Bahamas
161	31	Bahama Islands
163	32	Leave for Bahamas
171	33	Exuma Islands
183	34	Eleuthera Islands
193	35	The Abacos
201	36	Return to Florida
207		Appendix-Marlinspike
211		Distress Signals
213		Index
		Author's note to readers
		Order information
		Colophon

WARNING – DISCLAIMER

We used all available up-to-date charts for the areas covered.

The material in this book, however, is not intended to be a substitute for using current charts. Nor, does it guarantee the anchorages to be suitable at this time.

This book covers only conditions as we experienced with no guarantee that they would or could be duplicated.

WARNING – DISCLAIMER

The Hoekwater's

sailboat journey

Northport
Traverse City
Frankfort
Pentwater

New York

Waukegan
Chicago

Baltimore
Annapolis

Cape May

Illinois Waterway

St. Louis

Norfolk

Mississippi
River

Atlantic Ocean

New Orleans

Gulf of Mexico

Fort Myers
Dry Tortugas
Key West
Miami
Bahamas

Map showing our sailboat journey

PRIME TIME

1

"WE'RE GOING TO DO WHAT?"
"SELL THE HOUSE AND LIVE ON THE BOAT"

"SELL THE HOUSE and live on the boat?   Are you kidding?"

"Well, I am retiring, so we will have the time, and we have the boat and besides it has always been my dream as a young man to sail down the Mississippi River."

"I just cannot sell my home and go sailing down a River. It may have been your dream, but certainly not one of mine."

But as you can see from my story, I prepared for a two year cruise, taking a year at a time. Now I invite you to come along as we follow his goal to sail down the Mississippi, to Florida, up the east coast to Maine, back to Florida and over to the Bahamas.

EARLY EXPERIENCE AND PREPARATION – Prior to our marriage, Ken had several different sailboats and spent most of his leisure time on the water. Sailing was new to me and I soon recognized if I were to go sailing too and enjoy it, and to keep him from hollering so much, I had to learn more about the sport.

Together we took several sailing courses, refresher for him, and basic for me, offered by the United States Coast Guard Auxiliary. We later became members of the flotilla and since have held many offices within it, and continued to take additional courses.

11

We spent summers cruising on Grand Traverse Bay where we live, and also Lakes Michigan, Huron and Superior, and the North Channel.

After the boat is put away for the summer, thoughts turn to winter's snow and cold weather. He already has another challenge for me and says "it is time now to take up skiing". First with Alpine and later cross country. So, again we purchase the equipment and clothing, take one Alpine lesson and we are off on the slopes. At the age of 46, I am experiencing the thrill of schussing down a hill. The challenges and interesting experiences have continued since then.

Knowing Ken's adventurous spirit, I am sure the last boat was purchased with his dream in mind as it was equipped for living aboard. It was a 41 foot Islander Freeport, ketch rig. It had a 150 percent genoa with roller furling, mainsail, a mizzen with jiffy reefing, and a club sail. It had a "V" berth forward with head and shower, a full galley and saloon, and an aft cabin with another head and shower. The engine room contained the 100 horsepower Chrysler Nissan diesel and ten gallon hot water heater. We carried 200 gallons of fuel and 200 gallons fresh water.

The electronics we had were compass with an accurate deviation table, a hand bearing compass for taking visual bearings, boat speed indicator and log (miles travelled), a wind speed and direction indicator.

Also, we had two depth sounders; one was a digital and one a flasher. The reason for two sounders was the possibility of failure of one and the importance of knowing the depth of the water at all times.

We had two marine radios. Again, one was a backup in case one failed. Secondly, we could monitor channel 16, (calling and distress) and channel 13, working channel for the tugs and other commercial traffic.

The last, and perhaps the most important piece of navigation equipment, was the LORAN C when we were sailing offshore. This instrument receives radio signals which are converted into a very accurate and dependable fix.

After purchasing the Freeport, we sailed the Great Lakes another two summers, and all the time I would hear my husband say: "WE'RE GOING TO SELL THE HOUSE, LIVE ON THE BOAT AND GO DOWN THE MISSISSIPPI RIVER".

As he approached retirement, I could see his goal developing. That winter he purchased equipment and supplies, plus approximately $600.00 worth of charts, Coastal Pilot, Light List and other navigational aids. He told the United Parcel delivery man who was coming to our house almost weekly, that "many of these packages containing anchors, lines, hardware or books were ordered to make my voyage more comfortable". Thereafter, the deliveryman would greet me at the door with the greeting: "Another Christmas gift for you"

I FINALLY AGREED TO SELL THE HOUSE if the money would be put in a "house fund" to buy another once we were through with the cruise. All our furnishings were stored in my mother's vacant home and we moved onto the boat the first of June, 1982. The summer was busy making final preparations for a September departure.

And lastly, it is count down time for leaving and some more farewell get togethers: We were dinner guests of friends Bill and Marian Ragsdale and Bill and Gwen Baxter; Bob and Holly Goff and Mary Anne Friese aboard *SUNSHINE*, our neighbor in the marina hosted a party, and Mary and Orval Center brought home baked cookies, fresh fruits and vegetables, and 2 African violets. The African violets survived about three weeks after gallant attempts to recover from being knocked off shelves in rough seas.

Captain Ken wearing son-in-law Barry's lucky hat.

2

TRAVERSE CITY TO CHICAGO
WE'RE ON OUR WAY

SEPTEMBER 1, 1982 – *PRIME TIME* left the harbor at
1310 en route to Northport from Traverse City. Our late
departure was due to a final check of our equipment and
finding the LORAN C didn't work, the batteries were run
down and the engine wouldn't start. These problems were
corrected without difficulty and we proceeded to leave.

Our family and friends stood on the dock and waved
good–bye, and the employees of the marina and other
boaters blew their horns. Son–in–law Barry Boone gave
Ken his lucky chimney– sweep type hat to wear. Barry also
rode with us to Northport in heavy rain and no wind.

OFF TO A ROUGH START – Our first days out were not
exactly pleasant.

In the morning prior to leaving Northport, Ken
sighed: "The flag halyard has come loose and is wrapped
around a shroud. I will have to go up and untangle it." The
crew on *DOTTIE TWO* gave us the extra muscle in hoisting
him up the mast, some 50 feet off the water.

The previous night winds had riled Lake Michigan.
The three to five foot seas were erratic as we rounded
Cathead Point. They hit us from one side, then the other,
from the bow, and from the stern. We were able to get the
main and jib down, but with the boat heaving the way it
was, it was too dangerous for Ken to stand atop the aft
cabin to lower the mizzen. We changed our course to get in

15

lea of North Manitou Island, approximately fifteen miles off Michigan shore, and the sail was finally lowered.

You are not permitted to stay at North Manitou Island, however, South Manitou Island has a nice, safe anchorage. We were nearly there to spend the night when the radio announced the winds were due to change and come out of the northeast. This would have made a very uncomfortable night so Ken changed our course again and we headed back to the mainland. We had the option of going to Leland or Frankfort. To go to Leland we would need to backtrack a bit, so he decided it best to go farther down the Lake to Frankfort.

The winds were still 38 m.p.h and seas erratic. Due to the design of the vessel and heeling, three inches of water were trapped on the windward side.

And then it happened. "Ken, I don't think I am going to make it. My stomach is getting very queasy because of all these several hours of bouncing and jerking around." I try everything to keep from getting sick – looking at the horizon, eating crackers, but nothing works, and finally it hit me just an hour before getting into the harbor. It is a terrible feeling and leaves you weak for several hours.

What a day this has been. I am wondering what is wrong with my head and what I am doing out here, rather than being safe at home.

Because the high winds continued to be strong and nasty, we elected to stay in Frankfort an extra day which did give me the chance to recover and an opportunity for us to visit friends Larry and Joan Miller.

All this had happened and we were only two days away from home, approximately 125 miles by water but only 25 miles cross country.

The next day was finally a beautiful, warm and sunny day to go the 60 miles to Pentwater. It nevertheless took nine and a half hours to arrive at their Snug Harbor. Along the way, off Big Sauble Point, many fishermen were catching very large king salmon.

CROSSING LAKE MICHIGAN – At Pentwater, we wanted to cross Lake Michigan to Milwaukee. When we got up in the morning there were strong, 15 m.p.h. winds, gusty to 25 out of the southwest. These winds and considerable seas almost on our nose, would have made a very long and rough day to Milwaukee.

I was not especially anxious to spend another challenging day at sea, so Ken said: "Why not stay a day and night hoping for a wind change. We're not on a tight schedule and can wait for the wind and seas to quiet down." This extra day was enjoyed by going to church and visiting with the local people.

We arose early the next morning to find the wind had changed to the southeast and continued strong. Convincingly, Ken said with the wind on our port quarter, it would be a perfect day to sail. So we left at 0556.

The winds continued 15 to 20 m.p.h. with 3–6 foot seas. The closer we got to the other shore, the larger the seas because of the extended fetch. We arrived at 1610, 90 miles in 10 hours and 14 minutes.

In my opinion, it was a long and tiring day. Ken said it was a beautiful sail, perfect wind, a perfect day, averaging nine m.p.h.

SURPRISE – A Wonderful surprise was in store for us at Milwaukee. Coming down the dock were our good friends from Michigan, Frank Kollar and Bill Spinner, who had come down to the harbor to look at the boats. Their wives, Doris and Ruth, were in the car waiting to go on a picnic. They decided instead to bring their supplies and have the picnic on our boat.

Assembling the "A" frames to store the masts in order to go under the bridges

Frank is a very comical person telling about his personal experiences and had us laughing for a couple hours. He was so amazed and thankful to see us because he was disappointed he did not have the chance to say good-bye when we left Traverse City.

PREPARATION FOR THE CANAL–September 7–9 Our short trip to Waukegan, Illinois, was long enough for me because of the strong following sea. The wind had changed again and was now out of the north. This is typical of Lake Michigan as the wind keeps circling. If it isn't out of your direction today, it will be if you have time to wait a day or two. So we do some more household chores and preparation for going through the Chicago Ship and Sanitary Canal. Linda Sue Parks from Amoco, Ken's former employer, came to interview us and take pictures. It was their plan to interview us along our way. We were featured several times in the *AMOCO ALUM* paper distributed nationwide to all Amoco retirees. The Canal has several locks and bridges. One of the bridges is a fixed one with only 17 foot clearance. Inasmuch as we needed 53 feet to clear, it was necessary to have our masts taken down. Ken made three "A" frames, one for the aft section, one mid ship, and the other on the bow, for the two masts to rest on. We were very pleased with Larson's Marine in taking down the masts. They are a large operation and very nice people. Other boaters warned us regarding rough seas behind tugs so we lashed everything down securely.

Visibility en route to Chicago was only 3/4 mile and the 15–25 m.p.h. southwest winds were on the bow. We were very satisfied the masts and "A" frames travelled so well. In addition, we had our bicycles secured to the port and starboard aft rails, a dinghy on top of the cabin and fenders tied to the lifelines ready for going through the locks. This resulted in very limited open deck space.

19

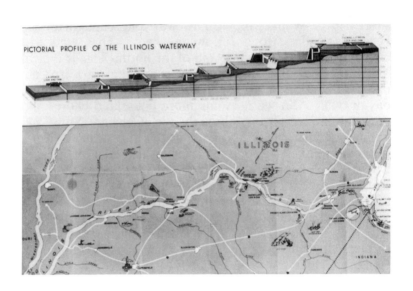

*Locking system from Lake Michigan to the Mississippi
River on Illinois Waterway*

3

CHICAGO TO MISSISSIPPI RIVER

THE CHICAGO SANITARY AND SHIP CANAL starts at Chicago and ends two miles beyond the Lockport Lock when it joins the Des Plaines River. Farther downstream, the Des Plaines River and Kankakee River flow together and form the Illinois River. The Illinois River flows into the Mississippi at Grafton, Illinois.

We were told the Ogden lock at Chicago was designed to keep the water from re-entering Lake Michigan. Going through this first lock was quite turbulent even though the drop was only three to four feet. There were no attendants and we floated free without tying to the walls.

There are seven more locks between Chicago and the Mississippi River. The drop varies from 10 to 40 feet, and from 590 to 420 feet above mean sea level. Attendants lower lines and assist in securing and give command to enter or leave. You may go through a lock with other vessels, except those containing combustible low flash products such as chemicals and petroleum products.

The sides of the locks are very dirty with grease and grime. We covered our fenders with plastic disposable bags, and used a long handle plumber's helper to fend off the walls.

Dorothy using long handle plumber's friend, pushing away from the slimy lock walls

CHICAGO'S LOOP AND CANAL– September 10 –
Our anchorage for the night was the Ogden Slip next to the Navy Pier. We had dinner aboard *PRIME TIME* and relaxed in the cockpit. At this time we fully realized we had left home, family and friends to start our voyage.

In our home town of Traverse City, the highest building is only ten stories. Here we were surrounded by the Chicago skyscrapers which were very impressive as they illuminated for the night.

The Canal winds itself through the Loop for many miles. We found this very fascinating. South of the city, you see banks covered with yellow daisies and walls of rock. Fleets of barges line the walls waiting for cargo or to be picked up by a tug.

September 11 – We met an interesting young couple with two small children and her mother, who was going as far as Memphis. They would continue on to make an ocean crossing to their home in Ireland. This was not their first trip overseas by sailboat. I admired their courage and stamina. We anchored along the Brandon Lock.

The Canal has many permanently built duck blinds and small boats. Water–skiers were enjoying the river and campers were using the shores. The protected water was good for the many pontoon boats and the houses built on stilts. The "River Rats Boat and Ski Club" appeared to be an interesting place. Young people were swinging from the trees and landing in the river. Trees were uprooted and laying on the banks.

SOUNDS OF TROUBLE – We were enjoying all the scenery and calmness of this beautiful day, when suddenly, we hear an alarm go off in the engine room. Ken hollered: "Shut the engine off. We will need to drift across to the edge of the channel so I can find the problem".

As we were drifting, a tug and barge appeared from around the bend and were heading for us. Ken told me to "kick" the engine back on momentarily to get out of their way.

In a few minutes he found the problem. The belt operating the alternator and water pump broke and the temperature had risen to 230 degrees. The engine room was very hot during the time it took to make the repairs.

We anchored for the night by the State Park on Buffalo Rock. It was a very pretty place with rock walls 20–30 feet high. The wind and current worked against each other causing the boat to circle. These conditions continued so at 2300 we set another anchor off the stern to stabilize. The weather forecast was for strong winds and a possible thunder and lightening storm. Mosquitoes were

23

everywhere each night, but this night there were thousands of mosquitos and bees around the boat. It was a sleepless night for me due to my apprehension of the anchor holding and all the insects.

PEORIA IVY YACHT CLUB – September 13 – Today we had an anchorage site in mind but we arrived there by mid afternoon. Rather than stop so early in the day, we continued on and reached the Peoria Ivy Yacht Club by early evening.

The waterway goes through several large lakes and sloughs when approaching the Yacht Club. Because they are very shallow, it is imperative you stay within the channel buoys. The strong winds made these shallow waters choppy and white-capped resulting in the boat feeling jerky and jumpy. Many cranes were standing on the sand bars.

We were 1,000 feet off shore on Peoria Lake and caught the aroma of fried chicken. It smelled pretty good as it was after our normal eating time.

A very hospitable dock-master, Don Buerschinger, greeted us at the Yacht Club. He offered the use of the facilities, including the swimming pool. The pool was certainly tempting, however, we thought we should get settled and eat first. Later we accepted their hospitality on the club deck. The laundry facilities were appreciated because it had been necessary to do hand laundry for several days.

Four fellows from E. F. Hutton joined us the next afternoon. They knew our home brokerage office manager and had a great time calling him on the marine radio telephone. We were their dinner guests that night at the Club.

We appreciated another boater, Jack Weber, a mortician, who had a car and took us on a tour of the city and grocery shopping. Prior to this, we used our bicycles to go shopping and to the laundromat. Later we rode our bicycles nine miles up the hills to Grand View Road overlooking Peoria to view the beautiful area one more time.

Our good friend and State Farm Insurance agent, Nick Nelson, in Cadillac, Michigan, handled our mail the first year. My dear sister, Betty McTaggart, in Traverse City, did the second year. We would call them every two weeks, or whenever we would be in a place for two to three days. They would then send our mail to us in care of general delivery. We received our mail from Nick while at Peoria and spent several hours handling correspondence and paying bills.

No change in our home banking or checking accounts was made. When cash was necessary, we would get an advance on our Visa card, and immediately send a check to cover same. This system worked very satisfactorily. It also eliminated the necessity of having great amounts of money on hand.

Our five days at the Peoria Ivy Yacht Club were very enjoyable. We have many fond memories of their gracious hospitality. The day we left, they had invited us to their pig roast, but the River was beckoning.

LEAVING PEORIA the scenery continues to vary. There is levy only and no trees for several miles, and then ivy growing up old trees and stumps looking like a jungle. There are many blue herons and turkey buzzards.

Our next anchorage was behind Bar Island, mile 86, a quiet place with only 1–2 m.p.h. current.

On September 19 we spent our last night on the Illinois River anchored behind Hurricane Island, 28 miles from the Mississippi River. It was here we see our first fairly large commercial traffic; a 3 x 5 (three barges wide, five deep) tug and barge. In contrast, we see the *GUPPY*, a small wooden houseboat on pontoons. It looked like a "modern day Huckleberry Finn".

Tomorrow we look forward to being on the Mississippi River, which I have now nick–named the "Big M".

APPROACHING THE "BIG M"– It was the 20th of September when the big day arrived.

25

My excitement is growing as we approach the junction. I tried to take a picture a mile away but, disappointingly, the picture did not turn out.

We found the navigation aid to be a regular red buoy with black horizontal bands which was no different than any other mid channel buoy. Actually, we passed the buoy on the wrong side; however, the channel was so wide at this point and no traffic was coming, it didn't make any difference.

I was so excited to be on the River, I jokingly thought there should be fireworks or sparklers at least to welcome us.

This junction is 327 miles from the entrance to the Chicago harbor off Lake Michigan.

We are now on the great Upper Mississippi River, mile 218.

4

INTRODUCTION TO
THE MISSISSIPPI RIVER

THE MISSISSIPPI RIVER is one of the major rivers of the world. With its tributaries, it drains all or part of 31 states and two Canadian provinces, or one-eighth of the entire continent.
The River starts at Lake Itasca in northern Minnesota and winds its way southward. Just north of St. Louis, Missouri, it collects the water from the Missouri River whose origin is the Glacier National Park in Montana. The great Ohio flows into it at Cairo. The River finally flows through a large delta southeast of New Orleans, and out in the Gulf of Mexico. By this time, it would have travelled 2,348 miles from Lake Itasca. It is interesting to note, that the origin of the Missouri River is 3988 miles from the Gulf of Mexico.
Where the Ohio River joins the Mississippi is the geographical division between the Upper and Lower Mississippi River.
Navigational mileage for the Upper Mississippi starts as Zero at Cairo and ends at mile 861 in northern Minnesota.
The Lower Mississippi mileage is Zero at the Gulf and is 953.8 at Cairo.

MY FIRST IMPRESSION – I was pleasantly surprised to see the scenery and activity along the shore. This dispelled some of my earlier reluctance to go down the River. I had been told by other sailors we would "see nothing but levee as we went down the ditch" which did not appeal to me considering my previous sailing on our beautiful Great Lakes.

The left descending bank was high with beautifully carved rock hills. We saw no traffic on the road below which formed the edge of the channel.

VENETIAN HARBOR – September 21 – Our first overnight stop was Venetian Harbor, a "first class" marina, at mile 213. However, they did not have facilities to raise our masts so we remained in our cluttered condition. Ken repaired the fresh water pump again and improved the quality of the drinking water by installing a charcoal filter. The current was only 2–3 m.p.h. and gave us no problem in tying to the gas dock to spend the night.

It never takes him long to get our bicycles off the deck when we get ashore.

We toured Portage De Sioux, a village of 300 population. There we visited the LADY OF THE RIVERS MADONNA. This monument on the shores of the River, stands 50 feet high on a 17 foot pedestal. The town is named for the Indians who came in 1815 to work out a treaty with the white man. It was a portage for their thousands of canoe.

It always seemed easier to prepare a meal when tied to a dock. This night we had chow mien and freshly baked chocolate cake. A little stray dog must have thought it smelled good, or else was hungry, as he stood on the pier and begged for food.

Up to this point, we had only met Jack and Vicki aboard *LA–BEL* back in Waukegan. Now we meet John, who is going solo to Florida, in a small sailboat, *SUNA*.

HOPPIES MARINA – We leave Venetian Harbor for our next scheduled stop at Hoppies Marina, mile 158.5, south of St. Louis, Missouri.

Just below Venetian Harbor is the Alton dam and lock. Even though the size of the tows and their frequency has increased, we went through the lock with only a United

States Coast Guard runabout, without delay or need to tie up.

In going down River, the red navigation aids are on your left descending bank, and the black are on the right descending bank. Ken saw a red buoy laying on the right bank of the channel and reported this to the Coast Guard. They put out a "Notice to Mariners" that *PRIME TIME* reported a red buoy was off course at mile 164".

We later learned this was a very common occurrence. Buoys could be off position due to ice, accumulation of drift, and often sunk or misplaced by tugs with tows running over them.

Large stumps or other debris can be seen floating and suddenly disappear. You might not ever see them again and wonder if they are near your propellor. Many boats, particularly power boats, get damaged by hitting debris that is below the surface of the water.

We used the navigation charts by the United States Army Engineer Division, Corp of Engineers. It was interesting also to refer to a road atlas which gave us a broader view of the River in relation to cities along the way and other points of interest which might be beyond the levee out of our eyesight.

North of St. Louis, Missouri, there is a large navigation warning sign that you should take the Chain of Rocks Canal instead of the River. This ten mile man–made canal circumvents the River rapids and dam. After going through a lock at the south end of the canal, we re–join the River at mile 184.

The left descending bank is now continual oil refineries, terminals and loading docks.

Arch of St. Louis – McDonalds' floating restaurant

We sailed past America's highest monument, the beautiful and famous Gateway Arch of St. Louis. A Jefferson National Expanse Monument by Eero Saarinen, it is 630 feet tall and made of stainless steel. The Arch represents the starting point of the United States' expansion to the west.

McDonalds have a paddle wheel craft in the River tied to shore. We could see it from a distance and thought it would be fun to stop for lunch. We discovered it was not intended for the boater as there were no cleats nor pier and the current was much too strong.

There has been no facilities for many miles for the pleasure boater. In the St. Louis area it would have been difficult to even find a place to anchor for the night. We were glad we had Hoppies as our overnight destination. You are again reminded that the River is primarily a commercial waterway.

HOPPIES – is a barge tied along the bank below the small village of Kimmswick, Missouri. The barge was very colorful with cleats, lamp posts, telephone booth and tables all painted purple.

Tying up to a dock with a current of approximately 5 m.p.h. was a new experience. You need to go downstream past the marina, then head back up into the on-rushing current. What is unusual when docking in current, is you need to use a lot of power to head into the dock and continue keeping substantial power on until the bow line is tied. In a situation like this, it was very helpful to have an attendant on the dock to take the line. The people at Hoppies are very competent and make your visit pleasant.

Near Hoppie's marina – visiting with Kimmswick's ex-mayor and his buddy

It was a strange feeling to have the water rushing so fast between the boat and wall. We were told the River is not really dirty but is brown in color due to it being so stirred up. I thought it looked like chocolate pudding.

During our short stay here, we rode our bicycles up a long, steep hill to get groceries. We met the ex-mayor and his buddy who told us the town used to be quite large, having "eight bars and eight body houses" and was an important stop before St. Louis. At present, the village and many 100 year old homes were being restored.

KASKASKIA LOCKS – The next day we reach the Kaskaskia River, mile 117.5. A short distance up this river is a lock and dam. We called the lockmaster for permission to tie to the wall behind the lock approach. (You need to radio for permission to remain there over night.) The lockmaster did approve; however, you must remain aboard as the dock is posted "No trespassing". It is a secure tie-up and quiet except for an occasional tug going through.

I had looked forward to fishing and dropped a line whenever possible. While here we each caught a catfish using my meat loaf as bait. It was many days thereafter before we caught any more so Ken explained that "the fish sent word downstream about my meat loaf being hazardous to your health". He also warned me about the catfish's barbed fin and how painful it could be if I got punctured by it. Well, the fin still got me and the pain did go from the fingertips to the elbow. He made me a "believer".

After he cleaned the fish, we played more Yahtze in the cockpit using a kerosene lamp for light and blankets over our legs to keep the insects away.

Ken holding our "real" Mississippi River Catfish. Bait used was my meatloaf

We were moving every day and trying to reach an anchorage by mid or late afternoon. The charts may show a bayou or island where you could anchor for the night. When you arrive, however, there may not be any water, necessitating going more miles to find a secure spot. It is for this reason you start looking for an anchorage early in the day.

Pleasure craft should definitely not be on the River after dark. The tugs travel all night. Their spotlights are blinding. The channel, along with its current and floating debris, is sometimes challenging enough in the daytime, and with impaired vision, the pleasure boater is asking for trouble if they sail at night.

CAPE GIRARDEAU – Sure enough, we found these cautions to be true the very next day. Our planned anchorage was south of Cape Girardeau. However, the radio reported the Corp of Engineers were trying to recover a large propellor and had closed miles 42–49 to navigation for three hours. Our planned anchorage was behind Cape Bend Towhead, mile 48. If we had waited the three hours, then proceeded to our planned anchorage and found it not acceptable, it would be too late to find a safe anchorage before darkness. We, therefore, decided to stop before that point and dropped anchor 150 yards north of the Cape Girardeau bridge at mile 51.5.

This highway bridge has a horizontal channel span of 653 feet and vertical clearance of 105 feet. Even with the height of the bridge, traffic was noisy and people would yell and wave down to us from their cars. The strong current and stony bottom made setting the anchor difficult. At least we were off the channel and fairly comfortable for the night.

A close watch was always made on the weather. This night the clouds looked like a storm coming and lightening was flashing all around us. In the morning, the weather was still unsettled, cloudy and cool.

Later we meet *SUNA* again and he told us he got caught in a terribly heavy rain storm with strong wind and hail the night before. This rain had missed us completely.

CAIRO, MILE ZERO – September 25 – We reach mile 0, the end of the Upper Mississippi at which point it collects the Ohio River and becomes the Lower Mississippi. The two together make a very impressive body of water, sometimes over a mile wide from bank to bank.

We have traveled thus far:

Traverse City–Chicago	350
Chicago–Mississippi River	327
Mile 218–Mile 0, Cairo	218
Total miles	895

5

LOWER MISSISSIPPI
MILE 953.8

IT IS NOW MORE OBVIOUS the river is for commercial traffic. Sometimes you have, on either side of you, enormous groups of barges tied together three to four abreast and eight to ten long being pushed by two tugs. These tugs appeared to be four decks plus the pilot house, high. You respect their size and inability to maneuver and give them a wide berth.

Mile markers are the same as for the Upper River. Buoys seem farther apart but perhaps this is because the River has become so much larger. The levees are higher; although you can see evidence of previous high water or routes the river had taken.

Channel depth of nine feet, and width of 300 feet is maintained. Extreme care should be exercised if you go beyond the nine-foot channel.

Therefore, great caution must be used when entering any of the chutes, cuts, or sloughs because no depths are recorded and they change daily. Also, it is wise, if not imperative, that you enter these waters going upstream. In the event of grounding, you can back off with current in your favor. Conversely, approaching with the current behind you could create a real problem if you ran aground.

The Corp of Engineers was constantly dredging the River. Also, they were placing large rolls of wire meshing along the outer banks (revetments) to reduce erosion or to contain the channel.

The two marine radios on board were certainly handy. We wished later we had the foresight to bring a recorder to tape the commercial radiomen on channel 13. When we had an occasion to talk with them, we had no problem communicating and found them very helpful. However, these people must have a second language as it was very difficult to understand them when they were talking with each other or giving locations on the River.

HICKMAN, KENTUCKY to MEMPHIS, TENNESSEE

PRIME TIME leaves the Mississippi at mile 921 to go a short ways up an inlet to Hickman, Kentucky, approximately 2500 population. Approaching the village, the flood wall is heavy cement appearing to be ten to twelve feet high. Because there were so many commercial vessels at the city wharf, we anchored in the bay and took the dinghy to shore.

The lower part of town directly behind the wall, looked mostly depressed; however, on top of a steep hill, the village took on a different appearance. John was also in the bay and walked with us up this hill where we found a nice little grocery store. After carrying our groceries and walking about four miles up hill and down, we returned to *PRIME TIME*. The three of us sat in the cockpit and played more Yahtze until *SUNA* left to go to another anchorage down stream. We must learn another game.

It is 0700 and Ken already has the anchor up, ready to leave Hickman for our next planned anchorage at mile 858, 63 miles away.

So far there has been no place we could raise our masts. Even if we did have them up, because the River continues to twist and turn, we would need to motor most of the time anyway.

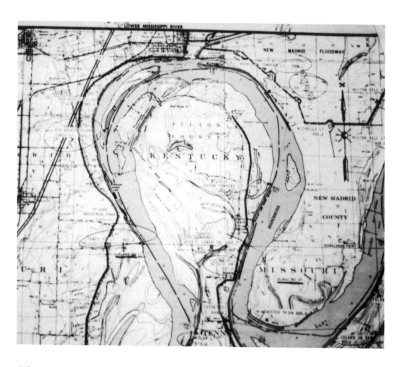

The River makes a twenty–mile loop around Madrid

We realize this more when we reach New Madrid, Missouri, where the River takes an interesting turn.

At mile 899 it swings north and makes a 19 mile loop, bringing you back down to within one mile west of where you started the loop.

There are few trees and no wildlife is seen along the levee. Many of our anchorages, though, would be near trees or swamps. Birds and insects would come alive at night and sound like nature's orchestra.

I am allergic to insect bites and had medication for it. I was told Avon's Skin-so-Soft was a good repellant so I used this lotion but the bugs would still bite me. However, I did smell good. So I made another attempt to keep them away by not using hair spray, cologne or much facial cosmetics. Still, nothing seemed to work.

The Monarch butterflies were on their migration south. Millions of them spend several weeks, as though they had a reservation, in a wildlife refuge near Tallahassee, feeding and resting, before crossing the Gulf to their winter home in Mexico. Amazingly, some migrate from as far away as Canada, a distance of 1800 miles.

I was told the legend that you would have good luck if a Monarch landed on your boat. Many butterflies would travel alongside us but even with my coaxing, refused to land. One butterfly did get trapped inside the dodger and flitted around trying to get out. I hoped that one qualified for our good luck charm.

It is another hot, hazy day as we leave for mile 785 to anchor up a chute near Osceola, Arkansas. A few buoys continue to be either missing or misplaced. Current is 5 to 6 m.p.h.

There were many barges filled with grain. We chose not to tie to any of them thinking the grain may have attracted rats. Other boaters had advised us to put foil pie plates on our dock and anchor lines to hinder animals from climbing aboard. We didn't do that but Ken did put screen over all the vents. He occasionally saw rats on shore but none ever came in or on the boat.

Other sailors told us of a possible anchorage on the Robert A. Everett Lake, mile 832. When we passed this area, we found it now to be an "inland lake" closed off from the Mississippi by a road being built.

The only pleasure boaters we have seen so far is one power boat going north, *LA−BEL* and *SUNA*. *SUNA* meets us again at our anchorage, mile 785.

SUNA was a shallow keel so he could get in many areas where we could not with our five foot three inch draft. He told us how the previous night he anchored behind an island. During the night the water level went down, and in the morning, he found himself aground.

We had been complaining about the *DELTA QUEEN* rocking us terribly with her paddle wheel wash. This same wash redeemed itself somewhat by creating a wake and finding its way behind the island where *SUNA* was aground. Prior to the *DELTA QUEEN* creating this wake, he had tried for approximately one and a half hours to get free. Then when the *QUEEN* came by with its large wake, he was finally lifted off the sandbar. He was in a very secluded spot and with no marine radio, thought he was going to be there forever.

September 29 to Oct. 7− During this period, we follow the River, going back and forth across the twisting channel. Current is increasing with occasional rapids.

Commercial radio traffic is also increasing. We appreciate the second radio in order to monitor such news as: "A tug and 30 barges filled with grain are aground upstream and have the channel blocked"; "the *CRIMSON DUKE* tug has ten barges floating free 200 miles downstream"; a boater radioed the Coast Guard that "a body just floated past his boat". Earlier in the week, it was radioed that a man had jumped from the Memphis bridge.

Memphis marina – when water level is down, you climb 84 steps to top of levee

On Mud Island, Memphis, a replica of the River, drawn and carved to scale

MY HOME AFLOAT

Captain Bob aboard his FREEDOM

Putting up masts at Memphis marina

On the radio, we hear that the River's water level has dropped another two feet and is expected to drop further the next three days. It's now more important than ever to stay within the buoys.

Approaching Memphis, we see more trees and higher stone and rocky bluffs along the levee. The occasional sand dunes remind me of Lake Michigan shore lines.

MEMPHIS, TENNESSEE, MILE 736 – I am really looking forward to spending several days in Memphis and being in a marina. We have been on anchor the last six nights, the longest stretch so far since leaving home 28 days ago.

Memphis has a new, beautiful marina and park on Mud Island. Here too the water level was down, and continued to go down a foot a night. The docks and ramps are floating, so when the water is down, you climb a ramp, then six sets of 14 steps, to get to the top of the levee. It was not difficult to get our exercise by climbing to the top several times a day. Some boaters found it necessary to climb the 84 steps to use the head and shower facilities at the top of the levee.

The park has several attractive restaurants and sometimes entertainment. You can walk along a most interesting replica of the upper and lower Mississippi River. The River's depth and width are carved in scale, notable sites and cities are designated, and landscaping is appropriate to geographical location.

An overhead tram goes from the island to the mainland. Boaters can get a complimentary ticket from the restaurants and harbor. We used this transportation several times.

We attended "downtown" United Methodist church services, the oldest organized group in Memphis, and first church of any kind in Memphis. They used to have 3,000 members, now 600, due to people moving out of the city. On this day, there were 120 people in the congregation. We met the Sunday School superintendent who introduced us to the minister and organist. They all invited us to the Wesley

46

dinner on Wednesday night. Their hospitality was very gracious and appreciated.

We enjoyed seeing Carol Channing in *HELLO DOLLY*. This super show was the last performance in that theater prior to its closing for renovations.

We again take care of neglected housekeeping chores while we have lots of fresh water. I oiled the teak interior and Ken cleaned the outside. We spent several hours handling our mail received here. We took the tram to the city to purchase groceries.

Later *LA-BEL* also arrived at Memphis. They rented a car and invited us to go with them to the laundromat. The facilities we found were good; however, we kept all baskets on top of the counter because of the many cockroaches seen on the floor.

We always enjoyed looking at different types of boats, and across the docks see *FREEDOM,* an interesting wooden trawler. When we went over to look at it, the skipper reached out his hand to us, and said: "My God, come aboard. I haven't talked with anyone for three weeks." He was a 71 year old man, sailing alone from Upper Michigan to Florida.

He told us of a funny experience he had on the Chicago Ship and Sanitary Canal.

FREEDOM had gone through the Lockport Lock and was looking for a place to anchor for the night. He called the lockmaster who suggested a spot down river. In the morning *FREEDOM* found himself aground. He called the lockmaster and said he needed water to float his boat. The lockmaster said he would take care of it. Soon a little trickle of water came down stream. *FREEDOM* called the lockmaster again and the lockmaster said he would again take care of it. This time, a wall of water came down and caught *FREEDOM* mid ship, pushing him sideways across the stream against some trees and on down the river.

Because the lockmaster and all the other boaters in the area had monitored his problem, when *FREEDOM* reached the next lock, they asked him if he was the same *FREEDOM* that had been aground. In jest, the lockmaster concocted a story and said: "I just received a call a short while ago from my sister in Chicago and she wondered what this *FREEDOM* thing was all about. She said everyone in Chicago had to flush their toilets at 8:00 because there was a boat downstream which needed water." They all had fun with *FREEDOM* that day.

At Memphis, *FREEDOM* was still picking small pieces of trees off his deck.

MASTS PUT UP– Ken inquired at the marina if there was any possibility of putting up the masts. The marina attendant told him, they themselves "had no facilities to raise masts as heavy as ours, but there was a boat owner in the marina who could possibly assist us". Ken called on him and the next evening the fellow and his son backed his truck with a boom on it down the levee and proceeded to raise our masts.

The bolted "A" frames supporting the masts were disassembled and stored beneath the saloon cushions.

Now we only had our bicycles and fenders on the aft deck and dinghy laying across the house.

PRIME TIME again looked neat and less cluttered.

The next day Ken tuned the rigging and bent the sails.

A FRIGHTENING EXPERIENCE – The boat owner who put up our masts told us of a frightening sailing experience he had aboard his Tartan 42 sailing vessel. A year ago he and his wife were in the middle of the Gulf of Mexico on their way to the Caribbean. Suddenly a flock of at least 100 black, raven like birds came out of the northwest and landed on their deck. The birds, either very tired or ill, got sick, collapsed and died. They scraped and pushed the birds overboard, cleaned the deck, and proceeded on their way south.

Some months later they were returning north and were in the same location they had earlier experienced the birds.

About 1700 they noticed the boat taking on water. By the time they discovered this, water was already above the cabin sole. It was coming in fast and they couldn't locate the source because the water was too deep.

There was no way to make repairs so they called "MAYDAY", threw the EPIRB overboard, grabbed a few belongings and jumped into the dinghy. Within a very short time, their sailboat had sunken out of sight and they were alone many miles off shore with nighttime fast approaching.

They were unable to determine if anyone heard their MAYDAY because there was no response. Apparently though it was heard because just as the sun was setting, they were rescued by the United States Coast Guard.

Because the boat was not recovered, they could not determine the cause of its taking on water. In addition, they could not understand why that particular type of bird was coming out of the northwest, so many miles off shore, and landed on their deck to die. Further, they wondered why their boat sank on their return trip in that exact location in the Gulf of Mexico.

They said the moral of the story is: – if a bird lands on your boat, you should never shoo it away.

This experience did not deter them from sailing. In fact, they were rigging a new Tartan 42 and planned to return to the Caribbean.

6

MEMPHIS TO NEW ORLEANS
INDUSTRIAL CANAL

WE LEAVE MEMPHIS with mixed feelings. We enjoyed our visit, but also realized it was time to head down the River to our next anticipated anchorage at mile 663, near Helena, Arkansas. We found this area also lined with grain filled barges.

FREEDOM has become our sailing companion, traveling with us and anchoring tied together at night. About a half hour after leaving an anchorage, I would radio back to him to say "good morning" and ask if everything was all right. Because he was always joshing with us, his reply might be that he had his boat on automatic pilot, he was in the galley baking muffins for breakfast, or reading a book.

I didn't mind and rather enjoyed, being at the wheel most of the day, whereby Ken preferred to be more active and free to keep a watchful eye on the engine and or sails, do the repairs required, and the many chores or tasks that kept coming up.

My handling the helm started several years ago. We were preparing to leave for a three weeks sail to Northern Lake Michigan. Crew was going to be me and grandson, Shayne Mariage. The afternoon we were to leave, Shayne's mother called and said he went through a glass door, cutting his hand, requiring several stitches and rendering his hand

51

useless. She wondered if we still wanted him to come, and we said yes.

About an hour later, I was leaving the boat and stepped off the edge of a concrete pad, injuring my ankle. Immediately it puffed up the size of a baseball and I was in excruciating pain. Ken placed icecubes on it, carried me to the car and took me to the Hospital Emergency Room. X-rays showed a severe strain. They wrapped the leg and put me on crutches.

Now what do we do? We have one crew with a useless hand, and the other cannot walk. Should we continue? My captain said "Yes",-- but because I could only sit with my leg propped up, I couldn't do the deck work. Therefore, if we were to go as planned, I would have to take the helm and Ken would have to do the deck work. This routine worked quite satisfactorily. As you can see, I am still at it.

Anchorage at mile 584 on the Rosedale bend. The current and river traffic is increasing. There are still no facilities for the pleasure boater and you find more possible anchorages filled with silt. The only animals we see are a few cows in the distance.

The weather forecast is for rain and thunder showers. This anchorage seemed secure; however, with *FREEDOM* tied to us, we both thought it best to set a second anchor.

The next morning, we got up at 0630, had a quick breakfast, hoisted anchor at 0700, and were on our way to mile 506, 80 miles away.

Yesterday's weather forecast was accurate. The electrical storm with 25-30 m.p.h. winds continued, decreasing visibility to one-half mile.

The weather cleared as we approached an excellent anchorage at mile 506. It was quiet and out of the channel. *FREEDOM* tied to one side of *PRIME TIME* and *SUNA* to the other.

Every night Ken and I spread out the charts and study them for the next day's travel. This evening while we were doing this, the radio announced another man overboard, mile 251. This is really not close to us as he is

254 miles downstream. We heard nothing further so assume he has been safely picked up.

A beautiful, clear, cool day greets us this morning with winds out of the north. We are well rested after last night's quiet anchorage.

At Vicksburg, the Yazoo River flows into the Mississippi at mile 437. Our plans were to go up the river and either tie up, or anchor, and visit the city. We turned off the Mississippi and proceeded up the Yazoo with *FREEDOM* following.

Vicksburg had recently been drenched with ten inches of rain. There were flood conditions, current 6–7 m.p.h., and logs and other debris were rushing downstream.

After a half hour of dodging this debris and just inching our way up the river against the current, we gave *FREEDOM* a call on the radio and asked him what he thought. He said: "Let's get out of here!" We, too, thought it was too dangerous, if not impossible, to anchor and decided to turn around and get out of there fast. And fast it was, as the current caught the bow and swung us around, we literally flew back down towards the Mississippi.

In reviewing the chart, it appeared mile 428, would be a possible anchorage. It was in the current, just off the black channel buoys. The boats were again tied together with two bow anchors. Water rushed between the boats. *PRIME TIME* was rocking so badly I thought I might need to tie myself to the bed to keep from falling out. Weather today was beautiful, but because of the rains, the current was especially wild and fast.

This was not the greatest anchorage and just the opposite of the night before, but the best we could do in order to get off the River before dark. Thank goodness we had a good sleep the night before.

53

Steve's marina (a floating barge) at Natchez

Washed out, rugged levee bank to Cock of the Walk restaurant, Natchez

We are now four days out of Memphis and on our way to Natchez, Mississippi, mile 364 with *LA-BEL* and *FREEDOM*.

STEVE'S MARINA is a floating barge with a little house on it, tied to shore and capable of holding several boats. Besides *LA-BEL* and *FREEDOM*, we meet *SEARCHER* and *LIL' GYPSY* who were also going to Florida.

The levee up to "Ole Natchez" is steep and rugged. The nine of us climbed the foot path for dinner at the Cock- of- the- Walk restaurant, famous for its catfish dinners. We sat at picnic-like tables with red checkered table cloths.

The bountiful and delicious meal was served family style on table service of tin pie plates and cups.

There is a special type of kinship and bonding brought about by the experiences and challenges we all have had on the River.

Our new little friendship group is growing. We first met *LA-BEL* in Waukegan, Illinois, *FREEDOM* in Memphis, Tennessee, and now *SEARCHER* and *LIL' GYPSY* whom we will continue to meet off and on throughout the rest of the journey. *SUNA*, who has also traveled with us occasionally, is presently some place on the River but we know not where.

PRIME TIME, LA BELL and *FREEDOM* left Natchez together and that night, with the lockmaster's permission, tied to the Old River Lock, mile 304. We all retired early and welcomed the quiet, peaceful night. No tugs went by flashing their lights or creating a wash.

We have been on the Mississippi River for 22 days and we all thought we had enough adventure for a while and were anxious to get off. In checking the chart, we note we still have 211 miles to go before reaching the Industrial Canal at New Orleans. Knowing the remaining portion of the River would be much more congested with tugs and freighters and lack of good anchorages, we decided to stay together until at least New Orleans.

We keep on the lookout for a 28 year old man in a 10 foot boat reported missing between Kentucky and New Orleans.

This morning is beautiful. The three of us leave for mile 210, which is below Baton Rouge. This 95 miles is a longer than usual run for us.

As we approach Baton Rouge, we notice increasing commercial river traffic, with tugs and barges, foreign ocean going vessels anchored in the channel, smokey skies from industry along shore. Many of the freighters looked in disrepair, old and rusty. We felt pretty small as we wove in and around them.

The River is much deeper here. The depth of the channel is maintained at 40 feet and a width of 500 feet.

The radio has constant conversation by the tug captains, which to us, still sounds like a foreign mumble. After hearing this steady chatter all day, it is a great relief to turn the radio off at night.

We had a nice anchorage behind an island so tied all three boats together, with *PRIME TIME* in the middle. This is a heavy industrial area with chemical plants along the shore. They gave off a slight odor and a low muffled whine of industry.

We had dinner aboard *LA-BEL*, then retired early.

We see Mile 132 in the lea of an island as the only possible anchorage site between Mile 210 and New Orleans. This night of October 14 turned out to be very memorable.

The evening was quiet and beautiful. Therefore, we again rafted off each other, socialized and dined together. *FREEDOM* was in the middle with his anchor down securing all three boats. They were on *PRIME TIME* visiting until 2300, then returned to their boats for what we thought was going to be another peaceful night.

CRASHING OF THE BOATS – We had observed several tows and tugs going up and down the River causing minimum wake. Because of this, we thought it safe to stay rafted together for the night. After a bit, *LA-BEL* decided not to take any chances, so he pulled away and anchored by himself. This proved to be a very wise decision.

We just got into bed when we hear a terrible roar coming from the River. We didn't know what it was at first but soon found it was a tremendous wave caused by a freighter. To create a wave that size, his speed had to be excessive and approaching his hull speed.

Rafting together in an area other than "Absolute No Wake" zones, proved to be hazardous and poor judgment on our part.

As this wall of water came under us, it raised *PRIME TIME* up and *FREEDOM* went down. Then it would raise *FREEDOM* and lower *PRIME TIME*. In the darkness, we stood on our decks fearfully hanging onto the shrouds, trying to fend the boats off from each other and keeping our legs from getting caught between the bouncing boats. Our masts were swinging back and forth causing fear they might get tangled. Our side rail came up and over *FREEDOM*'s rail, bending his stanchions and splitting our 3" teak rub rail.

Considering the circumstances, the damage was not all that severe. *FREEDOM* was able to straighten the stanchions himself. *PRIME TIME'S* damage was a ten foot piece of teak that we replaced later at New Orleans.

Miraculously, no one was hurt and neither boat received any other damage, not even a scratch on the hull.

Hindsight being 20–20, we now pulled our anchors and separated just in case another "hot rodder" came down the River. It was a restless, tense night after such an experience.

Our goal today, October 15, is Lake Pontchartrain. At mile 93, New Orleans, we leave the Mississippi and enter the Inner Harbor Navigation Canal which takes us to Lake Pontchartrain. This 42 mile run for the day would get us to and through the Canal early in the day. We were told this was important to avoid the rush of commercial vessels entering the Canal in the afternoon. As you know, pleasure craft have lowest priority when using commercial facilities, such as locks.

Going through the Canal, you first go under a bridge and through a lock which open simultaneously. Further on, there are four more bascule bridges with vertical clearances of six inches to five feet.

FIRST CHALLENGE UPON LEAVING THE RIVER – We were jockeying alongside the channel waiting for the bridge and lock to clear for us. We could see large rocks forming the sloping bank. Soon traffic had cleared and the bridge and lock were opening for us. I eased *PRIME TIME* into forward gear. Suddenly we heard a deep thud. I yelled to Ken: "I hit a rock". Almost immediately we lost power even though the engine was running. He said: "The water is too deep to hit a rock". He took over the wheel and determined the propellor had spun off and the thud was when it hit the rudder.

By now, the lockmaster was calling, "PRIME TIME, PRIME TIME, come on. We haven't got all day." We radioed him of our problem so he closed the lock and bridge.

What luck it was to have *FREEDOM* also waiting for the bridge to open. We called him as to what happened and that we needed help. He came alongside and prepared to side-tow us.

When we were ready, we called the lockmaster again and to our surprise, he immediately opened the lock and bridges. He knew we had a problem and apparently held the lock for us.

FREEDOM with the disabled *PRIME TIME* tied to it, a combined width of 25 feet, and each 41 feet long, went non-stop through the lock and all the bridges.

FREEDOM'S assistance didn't end as we entered Lake Pontchartrain. He continued to side-tow *PRIME TIME* into the West End Yacht Harbor, a distance of four miles. Many peoples' eyes turned as they saw us coming, still tied together, as he maneuvered in and around the harbor to the dockmaster's pier. And then, he again showed his amazing helmsmanship when he took us right to the assigned slips, a couple piers away.

MY HOME AFLOAT

Ken's dream to sail down the Mississippi River had been accomplished.

7

IT WAS A GREAT EXPERIENCE
BUT GREAT TO BE OFF RIVER

EACH OF OUR new "River" friends also had a problem now that we were off the River. They, too, were in the marina with us. It seems the River didn't want to let us go, or wanted to make sure we didn't forget it.

FREEDOM will repair his own bump rail and stanchions.

SUNA has a broken valve in the engine and will be delayed a couple weeks.

LIL GYPSY's first mate went to the hospital with phlebitis in one leg.

LA-BEL dropped a boom support into Lake Pontchartrain but was later able to recover it.

PRIME TIME's replacement cost of lost propeller, $400, plus $655 yard bill. This included repair of the teak bump rail damaged earlier.

    PRIME TIME was hauled out of the water to have the repairs made.

*Dorothy "supervising" replacing the propellor lost in the
Industrial Canal*

Ken assisting in replacing the damaged teak rail

She remained in the hoist's haul-out straps, not exactly level, with the bow lower than the stern.

We continued to stay on her during this time and felt like we were walking up hill, or falling out of bed. It was also high in the air, necessitating climbing a ladder to get in and out.

The search for a used propeller was unsuccessful. After several bus trips to town, we purchased a new 24 inch, bronze, three blade, left hand prop, cost $400.00.

The job now was to get it back the half mile to the bus stop. *SUNA* offered to carry it, but it wasn't long before he realized how very heavy it was. After that, we took turns carrying it.

We all had a great time in New Orleans, visiting the French Quarter in the day time, and eating at several seafood restaurants. Some enjoyed the raw oysters but I could hardly look at them, let alone eat them.

This was the first time I had seen so many cemeteries with slabs and vaults above the ground because the high water level made deep burials impossible.

All our River friends came to a delicious potluck on *PRIME TIME* the night before we left. Each brought their own meat which Ken put on the grill off the stern rail.

We would be going our separate ways in the morning with the hope, and expectation of seeing each other again along the way.

On October 28 we leave New Orleans to anchor east of Lake Ponchartrain bridge. The lake is shallow and with today's winds, it was very choppy. Our prop sounds noisy, but perhaps this is because it is new to us. We have a nice spot for the night, except for the ferocious mosquitos. I tried fishing again and caught three little non-keepers.

8

THE INTERCOASTAL WATERWAY
(ICW)

The INTERCOASTAL WATERWAY (ICW) is a buoyed channel between the mainland and a string of islands, protecting the mainland from the Gulf of Mexico storms.

The first day on the Intercoastal Waterway is more relaxing and scenic than on the River. Buoys are plentiful along the narrow and bending channel. Anchoring will also be less challenging as there is less current and seas are almost calm.

On a very warm, humid day, we arrive at Gulfport, Mississippi. It is time to do housekeeping chores again. Ken took advantage of the marina's pressure water to wash the salt water off the boat and bicycles.

We had anticipated and looked forward to eating a lot of seafood on this trip. I was still unlucky at fishing so here we purchased fresh shrimp for me and oysters for Ken.

We met many gracious and warm people when we attended Sunday School and church in Gulfport. Rev. Morris Thompson preached on Redbird Mission, Kentucky, which was familiar to us as our youth back home go there on a work mission.

The other minister, Rev. Harmond Tillmann, Jr. told us he had a hunting accident two years prior when a shotgun blast went from neck to ear, taking his ear off. He now has a plastic ear.

The man sitting next to us had no nose and much facial scarring.

Not a day goes by that we don't count our blessings and give thanks for good health and God's grace upon us.

We followed the ICW to Dauphin Island, the entrance to Mobile Bay, and enjoyed the dolphins playing around the boat at our anchorage. All along the Gulf there were many dolphins. Frequently they would jump or swim alongside.

As we arrive at the Rod N Reel harbor in Pensacola, there was an extremely heavy storm and cold front going through. Winds were strong and that night temperatures got down to the low 30's. I slept in a jogging suit, socks and piled on the extra blankets.

On the ICW between Pensacola and Destin, there is a bridge too low for us to clear necessitating our leaving the waterway and going out onto the Gulf. I was rather anxious about doing this, especially with the way the wind was. But found by staying close (one mile) to shore, we had good wind for sailing and fairly calm seas.

It shoals at Destin because of its location and there was a dredge working in the entrance. We proceeded to enter through the marked channel and promptly ran aground. Fortunately, the tide was going out so we had no problem getting off. After backing off and moving over a couple hundred feet but still in the channel, we tried to enter again, but alas, we touched bottom a second time.

We called the tug–barge doing the dredging and their radioman said: "Come over and I will lead you in". So we did, and we had no problem following him through uncharted waters, and well off the marked channel.

Destin is a nice harbor and delightful town. We enjoyed our stay. The next morning when we left our slip, and proceeded out of the harbor, we again went hard aground. Fortunately, a large head boat was coming from astern, threw us a line, and pulled us off the sandbar.

Normally in most harbors, if you stay between the dock and markers there is adequate water. This is not true at Destin, as there is shallow water in some areas along the dock (wall). We should have been aware of this as we came in just the day before, but we weren't thinking and forgot about the irregular channel in this harbor.

Continuing off shore on our way to Panama City, the beaches are the whitest sand we have ever seen. Tall condominiums line much of the shoreline. The cold front has passed and it seems good to be warm again as we approach Panama City.

Sunday morning is beautiful. Our United Methodist church was not within walking distance, so we went to a large, friendly and very hospitable Southern Baptist church.

SEARCHER came in and we enjoy the day with them. We made plans to rendezvous at Apalachicola and together, cross the Gulf to Tarpon Springs.

PRIME TIME needs some attention again. We purchased a battery and planned to buy another one later. Ken repaired the water and bilge pumps, and the one head which wouldn't flush. He also thought there appeared to be diesel fuel in the oil. He got the opinion of a mechanic who said: "Don't worry about it, plus it would take several days to get any parts, if necessary." So, we decided to continue on our way and keep a close watch. As it turned out, the sign of diesel fuel in the oil disappeared and so was not a problem.

November 9– Our last night in Panama City, we review our charts as usual. We see there is a bridge we won't be able to clear. We would need to go by way of the Gulf and many extra miles around Cape San Blas, then up to Apalachicola.   Ken said: It will be a great opportunity to sail on open waters".

But prior to Cape San Blas, and fortunately for me, there is a 6 mile long man–made canal leading from Port Saint Joe on the Gulf to the ICW.

If we had gone down around the Cape, Ken said: "We would continue going across the Gulf of Mexico to Tarpon Springs, Florida, rather than meet *SEARCHER* at Apalachicola." My heart sunk. I wasn't keen on this plan due to my previous, and rather unpleasant, overnight sailing experience, three days and two nights round–the–clock up Lake Huron. Needless to say, I was thankful for the Canal.

Apalachicola is known for its seafood. What did we eat? Seafood, of course.

I still have seen no alligators, only big turtles.

9

BIG DAY (NIGHT)
CROSSING THE GULF

SHOULD I JUMP SHIP?   I'm really thinking about it
because the only way to continue is to make an overnight
crossing to Tarpon Springs.   I am terribly upset with Ken
for subjecting me to overnight sailing, and especially on the
Gulf of Mexico.

However, believing we would have a companion
boat with us, and knowing his determination and
seamanship abilities, I decided begrudgingly to stay on
board and make the crossing.

Because we had travelled more miles, it was late in
the day when we reached the harbor.   In the meantime
SEARCHER and *LIL' GYPSY* radioed they were going to
Dog Island, some 30 miles to the east.   They would make
the crossing to Tarpon Springs from there, keep in touch by
radio and converge with us out in the Gulf later in the day.

Morning came and plans change again.   Frustration
sets in as we find our engine wouldn't start.   A hunt was on
in this small community for a mechanic, who after a long
delay, discovered only a loose wire to the glow plugs was
the culprit.

We checked our two life-saving emergency bags in
case we had to abandon ship.   Some of the items they
contained were a jug of fresh water, first aid supplies, fish
hook, line, floating flash light, signaling mirror, flares, sun
protector and hats.

We finally leave at 0930, two and a half hours later
than planned.

Later in the morning, we all hear explosions like a jet breaking the sound barrier. *SEARCHER*, still some 15 miles away from us and not in sight, came on the radio and said: "Are they shooting at us?" It was very frightening. The chart did indicate we were on the edge of "Danger Area, Missile Test Area, and Air Force maintained buoys". We could see absolutely nothing. However, we did hear and feel vibrations of the explosions.

Time goes by and we see nothing of *SEARCHER*. I am becoming more distressed at being on the Gulf alone overnight.

At 1800 we see two white specks on the horizon. Glory be, they were *SEARCHER* and *LIL' GYPSY*. At last we were finally going to meet. *SEARCHER'S* LORAN C wasn't working so the converging courses had to be done by dead reckoning. Looking for a sailboat out on the Gulf, is like looking for a needle in a haystack unless both vessels have LORAN C. It was 2030 before we finally converge. Considering the circumstances, we were lucky to have found each other in this large body of water.

At 2130 *SEARCHER* started having engine problems. While he shut the engine down and bled the lines, we circled him, all the time enjoying the dolphins playing around the boats. There was only a sliver of moon on this very dark night. It was still windy and the seas rolling.

LIL GYPSY went on her way and we stayed with *SEARCHER* who stopped several more times during the night. Daybreak greets us with early morning fog, and several miles of lobster pots.

We got to Tarpon Springs harbor at 1400 after 28 1/2 hours at sea. This was five or six hours later than it would have been if it had not been for *SEARCHER's* problems. I had slept less than an hour and Ken not at all, so we fell into bed at 1600 and slept until 0600 the next day.

I had survived another overnight sail.

Dorothy's transportation for grocery shopping and laundry

10

TARPON SPRINGS TO FORT MYERS

FEELING FAIRLY RESTED after many hours' sleep, we set out to tour the city. That evening *SEARCHER* took us to dinner in appreciation for staying with him during the night. He was still working on his problem when we left the next morning. Later, he found the cause – a defective line or fitting allowing air in the fuel system.

We spend the next seven days in Clearwater, Bradenton and Sarasota, lazily following the ICW, which winds itself through these beautiful cities. With no car, we toured by bicycle and note all the boating activity, both on anchor and in marinas.

Venice is another lovely spot, and with the low lands of Florida, it is easy to ride bicycles 12–15 miles a day to see a city. The closest restaurant was two miles away but we enjoyed biking the extra miles to the Morrisons Cafeteria.

The marina is more expensive than most and had no great facilities. To get to showers you walk through mud and oil. I always used the facilities aboard our *PRIME TIME*.

It has been some time since we have seen *LA–BEL*. They also have a home on a canal in the Sarasota area so we called them and were lucky to find them home. They joined us for lunch and took us on a tour of Venice and Sarasota. They wondered what we were doing for Thanksgiving, and because we had no plans, they invited us to dinner at Useppa Island.

Useppa Island is located 50 miles south of Sarasota in Pine Island Sound and just north of Fort Myers Beach. It is an exclusive and beautiful, privately owned club and island. Members or invited guests only are allowed on the island.

Cabbage Key is across the channel from Useppa Island. We anchored in an area just off the ICW in a protected area and took the dinghy to shore. After lunch at the island's only restaurant, whose walls were covered with dollar bills, we walked the nature trail. The island is very pretty in its primitive remote state.

The next morning we are awaken by two low flying twin engine airplanes fogging the area for mosquitoes. About noon, we pulled the anchor and headed for Useppa Island. When we entered the harbor, a boater hailed us to inform us it was a private island. We thanked them for the information, but told them we had been invited.

We had Thanksgiving Day dinner with Jack and Vicki at the old but elegant Collier Inn, named after the Island's previous owner, Collier, also of the magazine fame.

LEGEND OF JOSE GASPAR

*"Near Florida's coast is the small island 'Useppa',
originally "Joseffa", named in honor of a Mexican princess.
An 18th century Spanish admiral turned pirate, Jose
Gaspar, captured her. He made a pass at her. She said no.
If she didn't give in, he told her, he'd cut off her head. She
didn't. He did."*

Author unknown

(Author's note: It was a coincidence that several years later,
we purchased a home on Jose Gaspar Drive in Fort Myers,
approximately 25 miles east of Useppa Island.)

Florida pelican looking for a meal, a common sight in the harbors and throughout southern waters.

11

"WINTER"
FORT MYERS, FLORIDA

FROM NOVEMBER 26 to February 24, we were in a slip at the Fort Myers Yacht Basin.

Fort Myers is on the Caloosahatchee River, part of the waterway which cuts across the State, starting in the Gulf of Mexico, crosses Lake Okeechobee, and finally ends at Stuart and the Atlantic Ocean.

We plan to stay three months in the city marina. The occasional cold fronts going through make travel more unpredictable than other times of the year. By this time, too, we are looking forward to "staying put" and enjoying the warm weather of south Florida.

I immediately fall in love with Florida, its palm and banyan trees, and hundreds of flowers. I find fascinating the alligators, manatees, anhingas, ospreys and pelicans. Most of the waterways are lined with mangroves.

HAPPY BIRTHDAY TO ME on November 26.

While out riding our bicycles, Ken bought me a single red rose from a girl selling flowers on a street corner.

Later we went to lunch and our waitress hesitatingly told me I had "BIRD DO on my shoulder". How embarrassing.

She took me to the washroom and helped me wash it off. What a lady she was.

We walk the three blocks from the marina to the First United Methodist Church. We meet many wonderful,

77

friendly people in attending adult Sunday School class, and the Wednesday night family supper and programs.

Christmas season started with Santa coming down the river on a surf board. We brought Christmas lights from home. Ken was hoisted again up the mast so he could string lights down the shrouds. Many other boats in the marina were decorated with colored lights. The marina looked festive, but without snow or cold weather, it still did not seem like Christmas.

Being away at holiday time is difficult when you are used to being around family and friends. So we were fortunate we could enjoy Christmas Day with friends Mary and Orval Center, who were also wintering here and the next day, son Jerry Groesser and his friend came from Michigan to spend three days with us.

We went shelling at Johnsons Park, and to the Shell Factory. We went to the Dog Races; Jerry and I placed $2.00 bets, won $4.00, placed another $2.00 and lost. So much for that experience.

Several Michigan friends, Bob and Betty Johnson, Russ and Lorraine Spooner, Jim Brannon, and Howard and Agnes Darbee, visit and bring us news from Michigan. *LA-BEL, SEARCHER* and *SUNA*, our Mississippi River friends also share an afternoon with us.

The marina is full of "winter residents". We enjoyed many happy hours with Traverse City friends; among them were Les and Ann Biederman who spent a couple weeks at the marina aboard their *HAPPY DAYS*.

At one time, two slips from us was Jimmy Dean's *BIG BAD JOHN*. Dean was not aboard but we visited with his crew.

We have several dock parties – lining our food on the wall along the sidewalk – and oyster bakes.

Shopping was fun and easy, even though we were on bicycle. The downtown shopping was only two blocks from the marina. The Edison Mall, the largest in southwest Florida, was approximately 3 miles south of the marina. Several eating places were close by.

One evening we went to the Farmers Market restaurant, popular for its home-cooked food. We found it to be along railroad tracks, large storage buildings, and a generally questionable neighborhood. The hostess, when learning we rode our bicycles from downtown, and darkness approaching, suggested we "eat and scoot". She apparently didn't think we should be out after dark on our bicycles.

The speedometer and odometer on my bicycle are now broken. The last reading was top speed at 12 m.p.h., and we had ridden 523 miles so far.

Many nights I stand on the Edison Bridge until sundown still trying to catch a fish. I thought I was finally lucky but it was only a crab hanging on my line.

Most boaters sailing offshore, carry firearms. Up to this time, a shotgun was the only arms we had aboard. When in Pensacola, I asked an officer where I could purchase a handgun as we were going to cross the Gulf of Mexico. He said: "You should have thought of that before because no one should cross without sufficient arms".

Ken thought that was one man's opinion and chance of problem was minimal, but still considered it wise to be prepared in case there was a problem.

Because I was not a Florida resident, the officer suggested I buy Mace and still be legal. At Fort Myers, I purchased the Mace which I often carried in my hand or pocket readily available in case of need.

We still determined it wise to purchase two handguns so we arranged to buy two .357 Magnum revolvers. Practice shooting at a firing range was terrifying to me. Even with the heavy earmuffs, the sound was deafening. You can smell the powder and see the sparks fly. I had to use both hands to hold the gun and still there was the tendency for it to raise into the air upon firing.

CAPSIZE A MARRIAGE? – A few miles up the river from Fort Myers, is MARINA 31, a nice riverside restaurant having tie–up facilities for the boater. Several times we had taken friends on the two to three hour ride there, have lunch, and return to the harbor.

This time we have aboard friends Bill and Marian Ragsdale. When we approached the docking wall, Ken jumped off to secure the bow line. He started furiously waving his arms and hollering. However, I slowly, but surely, ran the boat into the wall, bending the chrome bow stanchion and breaking the running lights.

I had been anchoring and docking in rough weather, tides and currents, so why would this happen on a day with absolutely no wind and calm seas?

Well, Ken went into a tirade which lasted through lunch and our return trip. He ranted and raved for hours. I could do nothing but try to control my churning emotions and hold back my tears. Oh, I hated him for his long outbursts and embarrassment in front of friends.

Back at the harbor I started to pack my bags to go home. I didn't think I could ever forget or forgive him. After several hours of reconsidering this mess, and knowing this was not the first blast or unpleasant incident, and probably not the last, I decided to stay and make the best of a bad day.

The broken light caused a three day delay in leaving and cost $50.00.

12

FORT MYERS TO KEY WEST

TODAY IS BEAUTIFUL. It is February 25 and after enjoying our three months at Fort Myers, it is time to move on.

Before leaving though, we met Graydon and Bobbie Klopp aboard the trawler *GRAY-BOB*. We discussed future plans and travel and decided to go together to the Keys.

We purchased a billy club (for the big ones), crab traps and a pot to cook them in. The club was purchased in a sporting goods store but was considered a weapon. If necessary, we intended to use it to crack some knuckles or head of any undesirable, unwelcome person trying to come aboard.

Our trip to Fort Myers Beach anchorage to meet the *GRAY-BOB* was pleasant. The next day was a beauty for *PRIME TIME* and *GRAY-BOB* to sail down the Gulf to Naples. This "beauty" was short lasting, as it rained and rained and blew at 35 m.p.h. out of the northeast, and a coolish 55 degrees. We sat for two days on anchor riding out the storm.

HAPPY BIRTHDAY, KEN.

On February 28 weather cleared and we left for Marco Island. A south wind, puffy clouds and warm temperatures made a very nice trip travelling the ICW. The narrow channel is lined with islands, mangroves and bird sanctuaries.

DRIFTING ACROSS THE CHANNEL – The *GRAY–BOB* dropped anchor and we pulled alongside to tie up for the night. We went aboard to play cards. Long after sundown, the fellows noted the lights from shore were coming in different windows than previous and assumed we were swinging on the anchor. Lo and behold, this was not the case. We found the two boats, both over 40 feet long and tied together, had dragged anchor and drifted across the one–fourth mile wide channel, just missing the power line's concrete base and 55 foot bridge abutment. After separating the two vessels, *PRIME TIME* went back across the channel to re–anchor. We wondered why the *GRAY– BOB* didn't follow only to learn she had been pushed aground. Within a short time, *GRAY–BOB* worked herself free and re–joined us on the opposite shore.

The weather pattern continues unsettled. It seems we get one day good for travel, then sit for two or three days waiting for the wind to calm down. So here we are at Marco Island, again sitting on anchor weathered in by gale winds for two days.

To reach our anchorage on March 2, we leave the Gulf of Mexico and cruise up through the Ten Thousand Islands, a series of mangrove islands (all looking alike) in shallow water. Indian Key Pass is a marked channel from the Gulf, through the islands and into Everglade City. We followed the Pass about half way to Everglade City and found a nice anchorage just off the channel.

This area is part of the Everglades National Park with a visitor center south of Everglade City. Here at the visitor center, they offer boat rides, with narration, through the Ten Thousand Islands.

CROSSING TO MARATHON – March 3 – It took nine and one–half hours to make the crossing of 70 miles to Marathon. The Gulf was calm, little wind and temperature about 70 degrees. Water colors changed from beautiful blues and greens depending on the depth, the sun's reflection and the makeup of the bottom of the sea.

The Everglades' elevation is very low. Because of this, you need not be far off shore, before you lose sight of land. We were ten miles out – so much of the time land was not visible to us. This far out in the Gulf, water was still only twelve to fifteen deep.

As you leave the south coast of Florida the water gets even more shallow, though you are farther off shore. As you approach the Keys, and still ten to twelves miles out, the water's depth is nine to ten feet. In the Great Lakes when we get into nine to ten feet of water, we get excited. But here, we have to get used to having very little water under the keel.

On the way we see several fish, a green turtle, and coral reefs.

Well off shore, Ken said: "Let's get out the pistols and target practice again." After several shots, it appears I still need more practice.

March 4-8 – We anchored in Boot Key harbor, at Marathon, *PRIME TIME* again tied to *GRAY-BOB*. Weather was warm, and water about 78 degrees. Within five minutes after securing the anchor, we had our swimsuits on and were in the water. Using fins and snorkel for the first time was rather alarming, especially when you get a gulp of salt water. I am not a strong swimmer, and prefer a swimming pool.

Ken was hoisted up *PRIME TIME'S* mast again to repair the anchor and mast light. Then we find the LORAN C wasn't working. There is a repair shop in Marathon whose serviceman told us: "It is confused and has a poor memory. It is necessary to send it in for repairs". Because of the time delay, Ken decided not to have it repaired here. Instead, he re-installed it and it worked fine.

We say good-bye to the *GRAY-BOB*. They are joining another boat at Fat Deer Key and proceed on to the Bahamas together. We made plans to go with them to the Bahamas the next year and would keep in touch. We will go on to Key West. Weather has turned tropical-very warm and humid.

March 9- 11 – Our sail to Key West was uneventful. We opted to stay at the nice Oceanside Marina, on Stock Island, three to four miles from downtown Key West. True to the weather pattern, the wind howled for the next three days.

On our third trip to town on our bicycles, we finally got our mail. Pedalling in was a struggle against winds of 40 m.p.h., which they called a "weak front" going through. The return trip though was easy with the wind to our backs letting us just coast along with little or no effort. Whizzing along on a bicycle was a young lad using no hands, just holding his shirt out catching the wind.

Traveling and living on a boat, you learn from other boaters. Bobbie, aboard the *GRAY-BOB* made canvas bags to fit over their bicycle carriers. I thought that was a great idea. I had my sewing machine aboard so purchased some canvas and made them for our bikes. Each bag was made to hold a large sack. Now each of us could carry two bags of groceries. When not in use, they were folded and tied on top of the carrier, out of the way. This served us well. Wished we had them earlier.

March 12– At Key West we tied up in the old Navy submarine basin. In this basin there was a strong surge. Therefore, we had to tie to the next pier 200 feet away to keep from slamming into the dock we were tied to. Even though we were secured good, it was still rough. The water was turquoise and clear. We could see many tropical fish around the pier.

We took in the sights of Key West, America's most southernmost city. It is only one and a half miles wide by four miles long. Ernest Hemingway's coral mansion is now a museum. Other attractions are the Audubon House, where Audubon painted so many of his Florida birds, the Little White House where Harry Truman, when president, came to relax and Duval Street which has the oldest house, 150 years old.

Every night at sunset, weather permitting, crowds of people gather at Mallory Pier to see a motley assortment of sword swallowers, jugglers, balancers, bagpipe players, acrobats.

We attended Sunday church services at Key West Old Stone Church, scouted the old Navy base and picked up a few coconuts here and there.

While here, we meet *WIND STAR*, a Whitby 42, skippered by Dick and Ida Cooledge from Ohio and their friends, Roger and Carol Herrett. They also want to go to the Dry Tortugas so we plan to leave with them when weather permits.

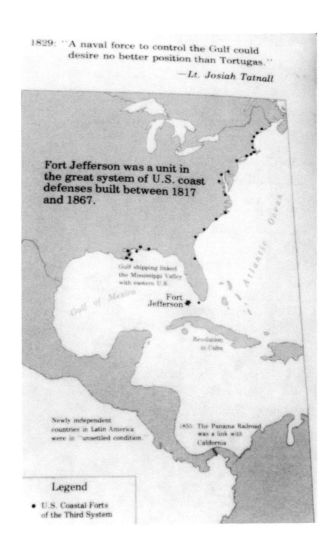

1829: "A naval force to control the Gulf could
desire no better position than Tortugas."

—*Lt. Josiah Tatnall*

Fort Jefferson was a unit in
the great system of U.S. coast
defenses built between 1817
and 1867.

Gulf shipping linked
the Mississippi Valley
with eastern U.S.

Fort
Jefferson

Gulf of Mexico

Atlantic Ocean

Revolution
in Cuba

Newly independent
countries in Latin America
were in "unsettled condition."

1855: The Panama Railroad
was a link with
California

Legend

• U.S. Coastal Forts
of the Third System

*Map showing location of Fort Jefferson – Dry Tortugas, in
the Gulf of Mexico*

13

DRY TORTUGAS

THE DRY TORTUGAS is the location of Fort Jefferson, now a National Park. It is approximately 75 miles west of Key West in the Gulf of Mexico.

It was originally called Las Tortugas (turtles) because of the many turtles seen there. Today, they are rarely seen. The term "Dry" was added later to warn mariners there was no fresh water on the island.

The Fort, built in the 1800's by northern handicraftsmen and southern slaves, has walls 8 feet thick and 50 feet high. Over fifteen million bricks were shipped from Pensacola, and tons of stone and cement came from New York. They added a moat around the fort for added protection against sneak attacks by enemy ships and storms.

But never was there a shot made from the Fort as it became obsolete before it was finished. No longer was the Fort to be used for military defense, so in 1863 it became a prison. Over the next ten years, some 2400 men were held captive in this military prison at sea.

The most famous prisoner of all is Dr. Samuel A. Mudd. At age 32, in 1865, he was convicted and received life imprisonment for setting the broken leg of John Wilkes Booth,the man who assassinated President Abraham Lincoln April 14, 1865. Dr. Mudd, after four years' confinement, received recognition for helping to battle a yellow fever outbreak there. That same year, President Andrew Johnson gave him a pardon. Dr. Mudd also contracted yellow fever and died at age 49.

There is a Memorial placque in his name inside the Fort walls. Over the door of his cell are the lines from Dante's "Inferno": "Abandon all hope, ye who enter here...."

March 14 – We leave Key West at 0630 with *WIND STAR*, and arrive 10 hours later. It was a great day for sailing, even though we had to correct the compass fifteen degrees to stay on course due to wind and tide.

We had been told you could have beautiful weather while at the Fort and enjoy swimming, snorkeling and seeing the many beautiful fish. Or it could be nasty weather whereby the fishermen come in to be inside the reef protecting them from the Gulf of Mexico open waters.

Well, again the weather turned and we had the bad weather during our five days here. Four different times we would go to shore, make a quick trip around the Fort, only to rush back to the boat before another storm hit or the white caps in our anchorage would overtake our dinghy.

During one period of 36 hours, we never got off the boat due to torrential rains and 35 to 40 knot winds, and briefly 50 knots. The boat was vibrating and the rigging was trembling. The line to our Bruce anchor was extremely taut. A large shrimp boat moored next to us had his radar going in preparation for a quick departure and said to us: "If this weather keeps up and it's necessary to take off in a hurry, I'll head off to starboard, and you go to port." Ken and I took turns standing overnight watch. After 36 hours of this, I, too, was shaking and more than ready for the weather to clear.

Pleasure craft bouncing in the wild seas in anchorage at Dry Tortugas

A fisherman came in from outside the reef, seeking shelter in the bay

Other sailors told us that in the event of bad weather, we should have plenty of beer on hand because the fishermen come in and want to trade beer for fish. In that respect, we were thankful to be prepared for this extremely windy week. On one occasion we traded two 6-packs of beer for 18 small lobster tails and 18 Yellowtail fish.

We hear the report of a fisherman falling overboard. His body found north of the Dry Tortugas was brought to the Fort's ranger station. They cordoned off the beach awaiting the investigators and helicopter to take the body back to the mainland. They believe one or more persons are still missing.

I think how terrible it is to know there are bodies floating around in these waters, and hope they can be found. On the other hand, I dreaded the possibility of seeing a body float by our boat and having to recover it.

After five days of whistling winds and almost complete confinement to the boat, we are hoping for good weather to leave in the morning. Key West's weather should be cleared after having tornado warnings for a couple days with reported touch downs in several places.

March 19 – *WIND STAR* and *PRIME TIME* decide to leave and take advantage of the better weather greeting us this morning.

As *WIND STAR* was pulling up his anchor, he got it up under the pulpit and within reach, when the pin came out of the shackle, dropping the anchor back into the water. The skipper was anxious to retrieve the anchor which would cost $200 to $300, or possibly more. He donned his diving gear. He made several attempts but was unable to find it because the water was not clear due to being riled by the wind.

On the way back to Key West, the radio reports another life jacket had floated back to the Fort's shore with the name of the casualty boat on it.

90

14

KEY WEST TO MIAMI
HEADING NORTH

OUR CHART BOOKS indicate   mileage at five mile intervals. We note Key West is at "1243 statute miles" and "zero" at Norfolk.

Cruising is not the speediest way of travel. For instance, at our cruising speed, and going "round the clock" 24 hours a day, it would take eight days to reach Norfolk. At our leisure pace, and enjoying sites and cities along the way, it took us 45 days to reach Norfolk.

It is now March 23 – We have sailed the most southern parts of Florida. Now that spring is here, it is time to head north. We want to be in New Smyrna, south of Daytona Beach, for a few days in early April to handle income taxes.

We previously enjoyed the Marathon area so on our way north spent another few days there in Boot Key marina. Upon leaving Marathon, we went up Hawks Channel, which is oceanside of the Keys. We followed it approximately 20 miles to Channel Five, where we went under the highway bridge, and into Florida Bay.

En route to our next anchorage we follow Steamboat Channel, which is part of Florida Intercoastal Waterway. Water was very shallow on this waterway between mile 1160 and 1155. We bounced off the bottom for three to four miles – it felt like a washboard. We wondered if it was going to get any worse and we would be stuck. We didn't dare stop. Fortunately, the water finally got deep enough to float without touching bottom. Rather spooky.

91

Our anchorage this night was in Blackwater Sound.

STORM – In the morning the weather report was "thunderstorms, possible severe weather". It was one of those days it just felt like a storm.

We were underway about four hours when we noticed the weather deteriorating to the west. The sky was dark and clouds started to churn. It was time to get the sails down. Bad weather was on the way.

At this same time we were approaching mile 1105 in Biscayne Bay. A reef, cutting across the Bay, had a narrow buoyed channel. Outside the buoys, water was only inches deep.

At first glance we thought we had time to get through this short channel prior to the storm. But then, we noted the storm coming at us with great velocity. The front was black, with a wall of water coming with it. Now, we knew we would never get through the pass.

Well, we did not want to get caught in between the buoys, or pushed over into shallow water. Ken took the wheel and cranked it over to make a 180 degree turn to deeper water astern.

With the turn almost completed, the front hit. Zip – off went the bimini. Ken grabbed it as it was going overboard. With no sails, we still heeled over 35 plus degrees. The downpour of rain was so heavy, we could not see beyond the bow. With the bimini gone and the hatch still open, rain poured into the main cabin.

We held our course with zero visibility and in about ten minutes, the excitement was over. The damage was a torn bimini and a soaked main cabin.

This front is similar to those we have on Lake Michigan. They can develop in a hurry, have winds of a high velocity and are over in a relatively short period. This particular morning, there was a tornado which touched down on land not far from us. After the front passed, weather cleared and the wind was out of the north, and fresh, which made Biscayne Bay choppy.

By this time I was very anxious to get off the Bay. We called Dinner Key, a nice marina south of Miami.

Because so many other boaters had taken shelter, they unfortunately had no room for us.

Directly across the Bay from Dinner Key is Key Biscayne. On this Key is Hurricane Harbor, a natural cove and excellent anchorage. There were several boats there but we found a spot to drop the anchor. We got out the sewing kit and Ken repaired the bimini.

The winds were still howling and seas rough. Several dolphins played around the boat. Maybe they, too, came in to get out of the storm.

This is the Key where President Nixon had one of his homes. As you enter the harbor you can see off your port bow, his helicopter pad. The harbor itself is surrounded by many fine large homes.

Thankfully, during the night, the winds subsided. About mid morning, we heard the *GRAY-BOB* calling us on the radio. They were at Dinner Key marina where we could not get in the day before. They said there was now room so we went back across the Bay and enjoyed their company for the day.

Early the next day, the *GRAY-BOB* was leaving for the Bahamas. We were heading north – our next stop the Bahia Mar marina in Fort Lauderdale.

15

MIAMI TO NORFOLK, VIRGINIA

THE ICW BETWEEN Miami and West Palm Beach has numerous bridges with various opening times, resulting in occasional delays. (If you are interested in saving time, you can go offshore. In this area, deep water comes almost up to the beach so you don't need to go very far out.)

There are several marinas and boating traffic is heavy on the ICW. Many boats were two to three times larger than we. "Cigarette Boats" came racing down the channel at speeds forty to fifty miles an hour. They didn't seem to cause much wake, but their speed certainly got our attention.

In some areas, the ICW has a solid wall of condominiums on each side.

Stops were made at Palm Harbor, West Palm Beach and Vero Beach.

The spaceship *CHALLENGER* was sent into orbit while we were fifty miles south of Cape Canaveral. It would be more exciting to be closer, but as it was we could see the smoke and trail as it soared into the sky. If we had been keeping up on the news, we could have been much closer as the Waterway passes within a few miles of the Cape.

NEW SMYRNA – Income Tax time – We will stay here until everything is put together for mailing to our CPA. Also, handle our other mail received here.

My sister and brother–in–law, Mary and Bob Lyle, who winter at Orlando, came over for the day. Part of the day was spent on the beach. It is hard packed clean sand which you can drive your car on. New Smyrna is an extension of the famous Daytona Beach.

Les and Ann Biederman on board their *HAPPY DAYS* came in to the harbor. They were on their way back to Michigan. Les was especially fond of the Take-Out seafood place next to the harbor. That is where we bought our supper and took it back to eat on *HAPPY DAYS*. New Smyrna is a nice, pleasant town. We enjoyed our six days walking the streets, going to church, visiting, and watching the many dolphins and pelicans in the harbor.

The fish market at the harbor had an amusing sign – with a smiling cow. It read – "MAKE A COW HAPPY, EAT FISH".

A few miles north is St. Augustine, the oldest city in the United States. We toured this interesting "old city" by bicycle, and also the 400 year old house, the oldest house in the country.

St. Augustine, like many cities along the ICW, is on an inlet to the Atlantic Ocean. Near these inlets, tides are higher and currents associated with them are much stronger.

Near Fernandina Beach and on the ICW, we were approaching an open railroad bridge. We saw no train, but could hear the whistle so knew a train was coming. We were getting close to the bridge and wondered why it did not close.

We proceeded very cautiously, and prepared to reverse if necessary. The train came right to the edge of the river bank, and stopped. So we carefully continued on through. We kept looking back and never did see the train cross the river.

Sign on a fishing shack at New Smyrna

The INTERCOASTAL WATERWAY IN GEORGIA is especially twisting and turning, with many very shallow spots. There are numerous connecting rivers, streams, and strong currents caused by inlets to the ocean. In the trickiest areas, there were ranges to follow. Without these ranges, navigating this part of the ICW would be risky.

While at anchor in a bay off the ICW at 2100 we heard a thump alongside the boat. We were in bed down below – looked out the window and saw a boat right next to us. Not knowing who this was, and in a lonely anchorage, I said: "Ken, get the gun, get the gun".

When Ken came out of the cockpit, gun in hand, he came face to face with another surprised boat owner – his anchor had dragged and he drifted back into us.

This was one of the areas which had a strong tidal current. At one time, the current is going in one direction, and later in the opposite. In between, you have calm water. Apparently this boat owner did not set his anchor for the current or changing tide. We never saw this boat again. We nicknamed him "Thumper".

The weather today is hazy and quite breezy, with mist coming in from the ocean. It is rather unnerving at the entrance of Jekyll Sound. The ICW buoys lead you to the ocean's edge, avoiding breakers caused by the ocean breaking over rocks and ledges. Outside the channel, the water white and churning, has a depth of six inches to three feet. We realize how close we are to dangerous shoals.

It is now April 17 – The day is dark and gloomy with threatening clouds. We were within 3 miles of our anchorage when Mother Nature turned lose her fury. Strong lightening bolts, wind, rain with hard hail like pellets. Visibility very poor. Because we were in a wide area of the ICW, Ken said, "It will be safer to drop anchor rather than trying to wind our way in between the buoys with no visibility." So we went outside the channel, put the anchor down, and waited fifty minutes for the storm to pass over and visibility to improve.

BEAUFORT, SOUTH CAROLINA is very quaint and pretty. It has numerous antebellum homes, a national cemetery, plus many other cemeteries within the city.

Boaters travelling the ICW usually stop here to enjoy the city and dock facility. We were lucky to see our friends, Joan and Mike Murphy from Lake City, Michigan, and be their dinner guests at the Beach House on Tripp Island. Mike was working there as a construction superintendent for a shopping center.

DRUG BUST – The second morning docked at Beaufort, looking out our aft ports, we noted strange events going on. We first notice several men, some in uniform, either on board or on the dock observing a 37 foot sailboat behind us. We had no idea what was going on until we noticed them carrying out packages and stacking them on the dock. The stacks kept getting higher and higher. It was hard to believe the boat could hold so much.

The newspaper item pertaining to the event said there were three men aboard. During a standard patrol, Customs agents asked them some "routine questions" and got some "peculiar answers". They boarded for a check of documentation and the contraband was discovered. Authorities said there were 165 bales of marijuana with an average weight of 40 pounds each, with an estimated street value of $3 million. The men were taken into custody.

U. S. CUSTOMS BOARDS PRIME TIME – Three days after the Beaufort incident and at Charleston, we have our own experience with Customs Officers.

I was down below and alone, when I hear a man calling: "*PRIME TIME, PRIME TIME,* anyone aboard?" I go up to see who is calling and see on the dock a white man, and a black man. They both flashed a badge saying they were from "United States Customs and wanted to check our registration".

Drug busts – U. S. Customs and other authorities unloading 6,000 pounds of marijuana from vessel directly on our stern

The one followed me down to the main cabin. Ken was down the dock a ways visiting another boater. I started to call him on the marine radio, but the Customs officer said: "that's not necessary". My adrenaline started pumping and I was getting nervous.

I showed him where the documentation number was engraved in the chain locker. After checking the number and our papers, he left, without any explanation as to why they wanted to come aboard.

Did they suspect we had drugs like the sailboat at Beaufort? – Or, did they think we were the Whitby 42, also named *PRIME TIME*, that was reported missing?

During the past week there was an occasional radio broadcast to be on the lookout for a 42 foot sailboat. It was of same length, having the same color markings and sail covers, and also named *PRIME TIME*, but of different manufacture. This boat, with two couples aboard, had disappeared somewhere in the Caribbean. Since the broadcast was made, two boaters asked us if we were the boat reported missing.

When tying up at Charleston, allowance must be made for a seven foot tide, the most we have had yet.

The bicycles are put to good use again as we visit the city – the Flea Market, Farmers Market, and wharf. We went aboard the *DANMARK*, a large square rigger from Denmark, used to train merchant marine cadets.

We spent a few hours in the "old part" of town, looking at the many beautiful restored, three to four story homes.

The next couple nights, possible anchorages varied from good to bad. The ICW at this point is close to the ocean, therefore, you have five to six foot tides and currents caused by them. It is low and marshy – with a mucky bottom. One time when Ken pulled the anchor line up, it was covered with crawly bugs. In some areas you look right out the many outlets onto the ocean. These outlets to the sea are too shallow for safe passage.

On the first day of May, at Wrightsville Beach, North Carolina, Ken's brother and sister-in-law, Gerald

101

and Joan, came over from Lake Hartwell, Georgia to spend two days with us.

On the morning we intend to leave, the marine radio advises the ICW is closed north of Wrightsville Beach for two days. The Marines at Camp Lejeune were having war maneuvers and were using the ICW.

When they re-opened the waterway, we proceeded north. There was still activity in the area of Camp Lejeune – remains of pontoon bridges that crossed the ICW – aircraft in the air.

16

NORFOLK, THE CHESAPEAKE BAY
DELAWARE BAY, TO CAPE MAY

AT NORFOLK, VIRGINIA, we have reached Mile Zero, on the ICW. From here north, you have a lot of protected waters, such as the Chesapeake, Delaware Bay, Long Island Sound. But other than that, you have off-shore sailing.

May 7 – In the Norfolk area, we stay at Tidewater Marina at Portsmouth. It was near commercial dry-docks. Big ocean going ships were being renovated and so the area was very dirty and dusty. We visited the maritime museum, and toured a Light Ship.

We wanted to go across the river and tie up on the Norfolk side but couldn't find a suitable dock space. They had a large harbor and dock renovation program going on. Because there was no safe place to moor, we elected to proceed north up the Chesapeake. Our initial intention was a five mile trip across the river – as it turned out, it was 35 miles up the Bay.

CHESAPEAKE BAY – The Bay was choppy, 2–4 foot following seas, winds 20–25 m.p.h. With limited visibility, it was compass course all the way. Weather threatening.

We found our way through the twisting narrow channel to Deagles Marina on Fishing Bay, a very pretty spot at Deltaville.

Soon after the boat was secured, a neighboring boater offered us a ride to town. This turned out to be a real

103

treat as there was a seafood buffet being served at one of the local restaurants. My favorite was the shrimp and Ken, the fried oysters. He found a pearl in an oyster but the waitress said it was no good after being cooked. Too bad.

This was such a pleasant stop, along with our favorite seafood, that we made plans to stop again on our way south.

Strong winds kept us off the Bay an extra day at Deltaville. The excitement that day was men playing with firecrackers, causing a grass fire in a field by the marina. Two fire trucks put out the fire.

May 12 – On the way to the Solomon Islands, we crossed the mouth of the historic Potomac River, 10 miles wide at this point as it enters the Chesapeake. Although George Washington didn't cross in this wide area, I think of that historical event today.

Going up the Bay, we were near a restricted area. Apparently we were too close because a Navy boat with two red flashing lights came speeding directly towards us. They told us the Navy would be using this area as a bombing range today and we should proceed to the east shore and then proceed north. This we did, but we were still not far off their range. We never did see any aircraft, or hear any bombings. Perhaps their exercise was called off.

The Chesapeake Bay is a sailor's paradise, with lots of open water and hundreds of safe anchorages, all kinds of quaint small villages, and large cities accessible.

One of the small villages is St. Michaels on the east side. During our two day stay, we had to sample the blue crabs at the Crab Trap restaurant. They spread the two dozen crabs onto newspaper, give you a wooden mallet to pick out the meat and you proceed with a messy, but good and fun treat. Still hungry after struggling with these crabs, we went back to the boat and fixed hamburgers.

Annapolis is back across the Bay and slightly north of St. Michaels. We were a few miles out of St. Michaels and rounding Bloody Point, as a storm front approached. The sky was black. Time for sails to come down and close all hatches.

With the engine turning over, and sails down, the front hit us with 40 m.p.h. winds, rough seas, heavy rain and zero visibility. You never know how much wind is in such squalls. We always thought it prudent to get the sails down and use the engine for control.

For various reasons, several boats made Distress calls. It was a typical storm front you encounter on hot, humid days. Within a half hour, we had our sails back up and continued on our way to Annapolis.

At Annapolis, the weather was absolutely nasty – windy, cloudy, rainy. We tied to the city dock in late afternoon. With our rain gear on, we visit Annapolis, its narrow streets, old buildings, Naval Academy, ship stores. Annapolis is popular with sailors and has a great deal of boating activity.

A short distance north of Annapolis is Baltimore, Maryland. Its busy waterfront has been completely renovated. It includes a fantastic Seaquariam, World Trade Center, and unique shopping and eating area. A large open area is used for various ethnic fairs and entertainment. Previously, the waterfront was a run–down, depressed wharf area in the center of town. (The waterfront renovation at Norfolk is being done by the same company.)

We toured the British HMS *YARMOUTH,* an Anti Submarine Frigate which came in for repairs and held open house.

The harbor is large with a substantial amount of ocean traffic. We enter the port along with ocean vessels going both ways. We stayed in the Inner Harbor at the pleasure boat facility, which is part of the harbor renovation.

May 19 – 20 – Son, Harris Hoekwater, is graduating from Garrett Seminary in Evanston, Illinois. Fortunately, there is a "National" car rental within walking distance of the marina. So we rent a car and make the trip to share in this proud and happy day of his life.

Still going up the Chesapeake Bay, we leave for Fairlee Creek or Sassafras River, finally anchoring at Chesapeake City near the Chesapeake–Delaware canal. This canal leads into Delaware Bay.

105

You go down the Delaware Bay to the Cape May canal. This canal cuts across Cape May and leads to the ocean. It eliminates many miles going out into the ocean and around the Cape.

17

CAPE MAY TO NEW YORK

MAY 25 – Continuing north, there is an Inland Passage, but in our estimation it is too shallow for us. So off–shore we go. Today, the ocean is about as calm as it ever gets, with only a slight heaving motion. We are two to three miles off shore and can still see the beautiful white sand beaches all along the New Jersey coast.

Atlantic City is also rebuilding. It has several gambling casinos. Parts of town are dirty and dreary. We took the "Jitney" bus to town for groceries. We thought our "hot rod" driver was going to leave part of the bus on some of the bumps. We toured one casino and had supper in a Jewish owned restaurant which was very good. We were warned by a marine policeman of areas not to go in. Some were right next to the harbor. We had a real good anchorage off the marina among several other boats.

May 27 Leaving Atlantic City , we hoped our next anchorage would be Sandy Hook. By mid morning the wind piped up out of the northeast. Although the day was clear and sunny, as time went on the seas were building. By 1400 we had much white water and were bucking into three to six foot seas. There was no immediate problem, but it was tiring and uncomfortable and we would not make the miles we had anticipated.

In reviewing the chart, it appeared Manasquan Inlet was a safe inlet and not too many miles ahead. Gratefully, we pull in there for the night. By the time we are secured, it is 1700 and still only half way to Sandy Hook.

We enjoyed Manasquan, a unique village along the sea. Many men were fishing off the rock piles along the inlet entrance.

I am still tired from yesterday but we head out again for Sandy Hook or Great Kill Harbor on Staten Island, New York. The tide was running against us but with little wind, the ocean was calmer and more lenient with us. It still took us 6 1/2 hours to reach Staten Island; considering the conditions, we could not possibly have made all this distance the day before.

18

NEW YORK TO MAINE

MAY 29 – It was exciting going up New York Bay and the East River on our way to Long Island Sound.

We sailed past the Statue of Liberty, Ellis Island and Governor's Island. We see the Empire State Building in the distance.

We continue past the Battery and under the Brooklyn Bridge.

HELL GATE on the East River – is aptly named if you don't study the Tide Tables. You want to go through this cut at slack water. At Hell Gate, the river bends and narrows dramatically. When the tide is running, currents of up to five knots and heavy swirls make maneuvering very difficult, and hazardous.

I had never been to New York and was "all eyes" at everything around me, yet staying alert to the navigating that must be done going through this very busy area.

LONG ISLAND SOUND – HOPSCOTCHING BACK AND FORTH ACROSS THE SOUND. Our anchorage at Hempstead Harbor on Long Island Sound, was at the foot of a high hill covered with beautiful, large homes. We see them intermittently through the "New England fog". We sat on anchor in the fog for three days, taking the dinghy to shore but one time.

Statue of Liberty

New York skyline as we proceed up East River

Sailing under the Brooklyn Bridge

Returning to our anchorage in our dinghy, we apparently got too close to a swan's nest. She tried three times to attack us. She would tuck her head and neck down into her wings, swim like fury, then walk, or fly, just skimming over the water. She was furious. At one time she actually touched Ken's arm with her outstretched wings. He finally scared her away by fending her off with an oar.

I am still trying to catch fish, now using cut up clams for bait. Maybe I should spend this "bait" money to buy fish at the market.

There are many harbors and anchorages along both shores of the Sound. We stayed at Cos Cob, Connecticut, crossed over to Oyster Bay on the south shore, and then back to Milford, Connecticut.

Because the channel going into Milford is very shallow, we waited an hour for high tide before venturing in. Another boater had not paid heed to the tide and water level. He went aground just outside the harbor entrance. He was high on a sandbar, heeled over onto his side. He couldn't be pulled off without damage to his vessel. To make matters worse, the wind and tidal current kept pushing him further onto the sandbar. For safety reasons, the people were taken off the boat.

Toward the end of Long Island is the resort village, Sag Harbor, another interesting tourist town. As is true in most tourist areas, everything is expensive due to the short season. There is a lot of shallow water near this area but channels to the harbors are well marked.

One of the many beautiful and safe anchorages on the Sound is at Shelter Island. Going into this harbor, deep water is only at the red buoy on your port, close along shore as you go in. About 100 feet away from this buoy, water is only one to two feet deep. Well, we didn't hug the shore close enough and went hard aground.

A small boat came by and asked: "Got a problem? Can I help?" Ken answered: "Ya, I guess we didn't stay close enough to shore. Can you take our anchor out about 100 feet into deeper water?" After that, all we had to do was sit until the tide came in and pull ourselves off.

113

In the meantime we were entertained with activity on the shore. Several cameramen were taking pictures of a girl model in a bathing suit prancing around in the water. One of the cameramen hollered to us: "Please don't move the boat. We want you in the background." They didn't realize we were aground and couldn't move if we wanted to.

Lighthouse on Block Island, overlooking the Atlantic Ocean

BLOCK ISLAND – is about 25 miles out in the Atlantic ocean off the end of Montauk Point, Long Island. The Waterway Guide says: "If you miss the island, which measures only 7 x 3 miles, your next stop is Portugal".

It is again necessary to check our Tide Tables for the right time to go through the "Race". Tidal waters rushing back and forth from Long Island Sound to Block Island Sound, in and around points of land, and around other obstructions, causes strong rip tides and resultant currents. Going through the Race at slack water is, therefore, imperative. Even at that, we had a compass correction of 5-15 degrees. It was a beautiful day. The ocean was rolling gently. And with jib and main up, we sailed at 6-7 knots.

Block Island has a large, natural harbor on the northwest side that we anchored in. Later we got dock space – off come the bicycles and we start touring the island. It was challenging at times as the island is hilly, with narrow roads.

CUTTYHUNK lies at the southern opening to Buzzards Bay and east of Block Island. It is the last of a string islands leading down from Cape Cod and close to Martha's Vineyard. It is a very attractive island with neat homes. They have a small harbor and natural basin which was overflowing with boats. It was so crowded we elected to anchor outside the entrance below a wall protecting us from the ocean. We could hear the ocean roar as it broke over the reefs.

Continuing up Buzzards Bay, we reach Cape Cod Canal. This man-made canal cuts through the base of the Cape, so you don't need to go all the way around. The canal has the large Buzzards Bay to the south, and Cape Cod Bay to the north. The effect of the tide on these large bays causes strong currents in the Canal. So it is again best you time your passage at slack water, or go with the tide.

115

Scituate, Massachusetts, moored close to Lobster Hut

We are now sailing off shore on our way to Scituate, Massachusetts. A Coast Guard patrol boat came whizzing across the bay, circled us a couple times, appeared to be writing and using the radio–telephone. We thought they were going to stop us, but suddenly they just sped off in the opposite direction with no sign or communication.

The bay leading into Scituate is filled with boats on their moorings. So many, that only a narrow channel is left to go in or out of the harbor. We weave ourselves to the dockmaster's house and luckily, were assigned the slip next to him. A bonus – the dockmaster also cooks, sells and delivers lobster. We naturally ordered two for supper that night.

Scituate, Massachusetts is a very quaint New England town. Many colorful homes on narrow streets – cottages on the ocean. The smell of sea is strong. Ten foot tide here.

It is June 13 and we are sailing offshore, heading for Gloucester, Mass. Strictly a LORAN C and compass day – Fog and haze. Ken reminds me again: "The scenery up here is beautiful"; but I don't see it from offshore.

The ocean remains a gentle rolling action with small swells. With no wind to fill the sails, it is motoring all the way. We anchored in Gloucester harbor protected by the break water wall and Eastern Point.

In the morning, Ken pulled the anchor and we took off with weather and visibility the same as yesterday – fog, haze and calm seas. Next stop will be Maine.

117

PRIME TIME hauled out for bottom paint

19

MAINE

PERMISSION was given us to tie to a mooring in Pepperrell Cove, Kittery Point, Maine, across the river from Portsmouth, New Hampshire. After being at sea for several hours, the dinghy is launched in a hurry, and we head for shore. Surprise, the fog and haze are not over land, and on shore it is now beautiful. Ken was right about the scenery, even though I did not see it from the water. We visited the one and only grocery store, toured a fort and meandered around.

On our way to Portland it is another day of fog and haze, visibility one-half to two miles, ocean has a gentle rolling action. In this area the LORAN C is very accurate in pin-pointing your location. It was especially appreciated and helpful in this continual poor visibility. At one point, Ken was standing at the bow trying to see the buoys through the fog. He could hear the buoy gong. In fog, however, sounds are sometimes distorted. At the last minute, he saw the buoy and called: "Alter your course to starboard. The buoy is dead ahead." The buoy appeared right where the LORAN C showed it to be. Without a change in course, we might have collided with it.

Rain and thunder showers are predicted for tonight. Only a few fishing boats are seen – could others be out in the fog? I'm still waiting to see the shore from the water. We note most pleasure boats have radar. In this fog it would be a real advantage.

Portland, population 70,000 is the largest city in Maine. It too has the odor of the sea. We tie to a floating dock and today it is bouncing up and down. The eight foot tide is out, leaving the pier posts towering high in the air. Each time you go ashore, you need to climb several rickety steps. Several old wharves and old, old buildings line the shore. Boones restaurant, one of several on the waterfront, was our favorite for seafood.

By this time I need a haircut and a permanent. I selected a salon which apparently specialized with customers still wanting "finger waves and pin curls". I wasn't pleased but maybe it will improve, otherwise I will need a short haircut. Speaking of haircuts, Ken also went to a barber. He almost changed his mind while waiting his turn. The previous customer had a full beard and wanted "just a trim". He ended up with a short "Van Dyke". When Ken finally got into the chair, he told the barber what he wanted, and the barber replied: "I know just what you want." When he got done, he was pretty well clipped, but not as bad as I had expected.

The fog continues to roll in.

BOOTHBAY HARBOR, MAINE – June 17/22 – Not far off the coastline of Maine are many islands. Unfortunately, it was another very foggy day, zero to 1/2 mile visibility, so I continue to ask: "When will I see the beautiful shore of Maine from the water?" The channel buoys into Boothbay Harbor were lost in the thick fog. As we were feeling our way through the fog, a fishing boat passed a couple hundred feet to our starboard. Knowing he had radar, we fell in behind and kept him sight. As we got farther into the harbor, and away from the ocean, visibility improved to the point it was clear by the time we got to the dock. Again, the fog was over the ocean, and on shore it was a beautiful clear day. The ocean was calm, except for its constant heaving and rolling.

The Maine natives ("Mainers") told us they "make fog" here. They made me a believer.

Tides are 8–10 foot here. When the tide is out, the walkway up from the floating docks is very steep and sometimes wobbly. That is when you also see many starfish and crabs hanging on the posts.

Downtown Boothbay Harbor is resort oriented, many restaurants, ice cream cafes, taffy pulls, clothing and souvenir shops. Lilacs are in bloom, many rock gardens with petunias and marigolds. Streets are very narrow, winding, and up and down steep hills.

We expected to get our mail here at Boothbay Harbor. We learned, however, there was another "Boothbay" and "East Boothbay", each having a post office. So on our bikes we go to make the rounds to find our mail. Ken could handle the hills, but I huffed and puffed the 3 1/2 miles to East Boothbay. We finally got there, but our mail was not there. The next afternoon, still weary from yesterday, we make a second trip and this time we got our mail.

Maine lobsters – what a delicacy and something we had been looking forward to having. At the outdoor cookeries, you select a live small, medium or large lobster from tanks of water. They put it in a numbered mesh bag and boil it. When ready, your number is called to pick up your delicious lobster, hot butter and corn on the cob. You sit at picnic tables, or some places have a screened–in table area.

Other delectables can be ordered too – clams, which Ken enjoyed, french fries, cold slaw and drinks.

We went to church and noted 95 percent in attendance were women. Their regular pastor, also a woman, was not there that day.

The marine radio reported the *TANYA MARIA* is having torpedo exercises and all boats should stay a mile away. Following is a newspaper clipping:

"Netted" torpedo falls back into ocean. *A torpedo, picked up off Maine yesterday in a fishing net, slipped back into the ocean before a Navy bomb squad arrived to defuse it, the Coast Guard said. Officials said they received a report about 3 a.m. that the TANYA MARIA had snagged a torpedo about 35 miles south of Boothbay Harbor. An explosion ordnance team was sent from Brunswick Naval Air Station to the boat, but before the vessel arrived, the torpedo apparently fell out of the net as it was being haul aboard by the three—man fishing boat crew."*

20

MOUNT KATAHDIN
BAXTER STATE PARK

DAUGHTER Jean Hoekwater Gordon had wanted us to sail Maine waters for years. Our timing was not good, as she had accepted a summer job in Labrador and to satisfy her contract, had to leave prior to our arriving. Her husband, John, a park ranger and whom we had not yet met, was left to entertain us. He wanted us to spend time at his ranger cabin at Chimney Pond in Baxter State Park on Mount Katahdin. Since then, Jean has become the naturalist at the park.

Governor Baxter purchased this park land with his own private funds and dedicated it to the people of Maine, along with a trust fund for its operating expenses. His terms were that it be kept forever in its primitive, natural state.

Governor Baxter would probably be happy to see how his park is being taken care of. It is a very scenic area and is very popular with the camper and hiker. There are only a limited number of people allowed in the park at one time, so advanced reservations are necessary.

ON TO THE MOUNTAIN – The day John was to pick us up at the boat, he was delayed. It was 0030 before he arrived.

We arrived at their home in Greenville at 0400, slept for a few hours, then proceeded to the mountain.

123

Map of Maine. Baxter State Park is the shaded area in northern Maine

The beauty of Maine makes up for its lack of population. We passed Moosehead Lake, largest fresh water lake in the state, Squaw Mountain, a large ski area, Canadian mountains in the distance, "Moose" crossing signs , deer alongside, and cows in the roadway.

The closest parking place to John's cabin at Chimney Pond is the Roaring Brook campground, elevation 1500 feet. Here we leave his car.

I used the outdoor toilet facilities. The outside latch on the door was flawed, and much to my surprise, once you close the door, the latch fell closed and I was locked in. Ken heard my plea: "Help, help, get me out of here." Fortunately, he was close enough to hear my yell and opened the door.

We gather up our gear and proceed to climb for 3.3 miles, over stones, rocks, foot bridges and streams, to his ranger cabin, elevation 2914 feet.   The mountain top elevation is 5267 feet, and is the second highest point in New England.

All supplies need to be carried in and back out. John and Ken carried the largest backpacks. My smaller one was enough for me. I had a hat and full head mosquito netting, and covered with bug spray, and those black flies still got me.

It was 2100 and quite dark in the woods when we reached his cabin.

Chimney Pond, a beautiful pond surrounded by mountains was a gorgeous sight and well worth the effort getting there.

We enjoyed five days with John. His cabin was modest, but comfortable, one bedroom, living/kitchen, wood heat, propane cooking, outdoor toilet. The metal shower stall in the bedroom had the only hot water. Very accommodating for being in such a remote area.

We hiked several of the trails until the boulders got so large I would be on my hands and knees going over them. After that, I stayed in camp. Ken said: "I want to do it all", so he continued to go with John to the mountain top.

While at the cabin that day, a huge bull moose hung around the front door. He actually appeared to be posing for pictures. A year old calf came near also. I thought some of the campers who came to take pictures, got dangerously close. John emphasized later: "Remember these are wild animals. Stay your distance and if encountered on a trail, give them the right of way."

Moose outside our cabin, appearing to be posed for pictures

John and Dorothy with their back packs, hiking up Mt. Katahdin over logs, rocks and foot bridges

127

John's ranger cabin at Chimney Pond on Mt. Katahdin

Hiking below the steep cliffs of Mt. Katahdin

Our experience of staying on the mountain has come to an end. We prepare our backpacks, gather all the trash, and start down the mountain. I find going down not as strenuous. Yet, with my trifocal glasses, I still had to watch every step.

Going back to the boat, John said: "I'd like to give you a short tour of Maine". We drove by where he and Jean go white-water rafting, the College of Atlantic where Jean went to school and where they were married, Mt. Desert, the cities of Rockland, Camden and Rockport. We stopped for groceries and got to the harbor at 2100, after dark.

21

TRYING TO GET BACK TO THE BOAT

DURING THE TIME we were on the mountain, *PRIME TIME* was pulled for bottom painting. They were instructed to put her back on a mooring and leave the dinghy on shore for when we returned.

To our dismay, we found the dinghy was still on the boat and both were on a mooring not visible in the darkness of night.

Now what do I do?

Ken said: "We will get out to the boat". In his determination, he "borrowed" a dinghy tied to the dock, put us and the groceries in it. It was incoming tide and the current strong. It immediately pushed us across big rocks and caught us on the railroad track used to haul out boats. I said: "Get me back to the dock. We're not getting any place." Returning was another screaming experience, as he would paddle one way, and I would another.

Ken looked around and found another dinghy. This time the paper sacks holding the groceries got wet and everything spilled out. John, still standing by and watching this fiasco said: "I have some plastic bags in my car." He got several bags from his car and we re-packaged the groceries.

Three times and out? Ken insisted on trying again by taking a rubber raft.   I am very upset with him by this time and refuse to get in the raft.

131

It was a good thing, too, as the raft was partially deflated. The weight of him and the groceries nearly caved it in. He got 50 feet out in the incoming tide and could go no further.

By this time in exasperation, I declare: "I have had it. I'm going to a motel." I gather up a few things and start my way up the rickety, swinging steps. But still he said: "Just wait a minute – I'll find us a place to stay."

He took a flashlight and looked down into a fishing boat also tied to the dock. The open cockpit had floorboards out – it was apparently being worked on. The cutty cabin had 2 bunks. He said: "Here it is, I found it, it will be out of the weather, and no one around," – so we crawled in to spend the night.

Before long, I got cold. He found a large of piece of folded canvas in the cockpit, and stretched that across to cover both bunks.

Soon after getting re–settled in our bunks, we are awakened by a loud noise. "What was that? Has the owner of the boat come aboard? Will we be untied and towed away?" "Will we be arrested?"

We charge out of bed, cautiously crawl out of the cabin, wondering what we will face.

An enormous sigh of relief – we find it was the bilge pump motor. There was a hose from the bilge pumping water overboard. Thereafter I kept my ears tuned to it coming on again, but it didn't. Also in my weariness, I kept my eye on a sailboat secured behind us, thinking that if they went up and we went down, we were sinking.

Daylight breaks at 0430 and in the haze, we can see *PRIME TIME* on her mooring. It is too far to swim, and we still have several bags of groceries. Ken said: "There has to be a way to get out there." He looked around and found another dinghy at the pier. This one had a motor, which he was able to start. We load up our groceries, get in and take off for *PRIME TIME*.

He then towed our dinghy back to return the "borrowed" one to complete a very frustrating night.

The next day there is a boat parade. The harbor is overflowing with various sizes and kinds of vessels. A motorized barge filled with dozens of partying young people and a band cruised in front of us. One young man had the audacity to relieve himself off the stern as they passed by.

Upon waking in the morning we are socked in again with thick fog. We sit on the mooring for three days, in near zero visibility. We had wanted to visit Rockland and Camden before turning back. But because John drove us through these cities, and more importantly, the marine radio said "more fog to come", we decided to start our return south as soon as visibility improved.

22

RETURN TRIP SOUTH
MAINE TO CAPE COD CANAL

TODAY IS JULY 4th – Independence Day . A day of freedom and such an appropriate day for us to realize that it is possible to fulfill a dream and reach your goal.

We plan to visit different cities on the way south, and re–visit others.

Ken is up early this morning, checking the weather. He wakes me up and says: "Visibility has improved enough so let's get ready to leave for Portland". There was no fog but a heavy haze over the ocean so you couldn't tell the water from the sky. He hoisted the anchor, we stowed everything away, and pointed *PRIME TIME* southward.

We roll up and down the swells of the ocean. By mid morning, the haze has cleared, increasing visibility to several miles. We see land for the first time from the sea. Several, very large whales came slowly and beautifully up out of the water. They were a few hundred yards away. I wondered if such a mammal could capsize us.

The wind has picked up considerably as we approach the Portland Harbor.

PORTLAND – We were given the one vacant slip, which the dockmaster said: "belonged to a fisherman who was out for a few days". But late that afternoon, the fisherman did return and wanted his slip.

135

We had no alternative but to leave the harbor and tie alongside the outside wall. The wind is now a steady 20 knots, not the best conditions for maneuvering in close quarters. The fisherman kept telling us: "No problem, no problem".

We weave our way through several large tuna boats, whose bow sprits hung out at least a dozen feet. Ken is on the bow ready to throw a line, or jump off onto the dock. At the same time, I would ease the nose in, turn the wheel hard to port, and the stern pulled itself alongside the wall. There were only inches to spare fore and aft. Several boatmen were standing on the dock. They were "amazed at seeing a woman handling a boat", and called their wives down to show them what I had done. The fisherman said: "See, I told you, – No problem".

The fisherman gave us a tour of his very old, dirty, wood fishing boat and also a lesson on filleting fish. He was chewing tobacco and drinking liquor from a bottle. He planned to go fishing when his crewmate wife arrived. I don't know what a "fisherman's wife should look like", but I was certainly surprised to see how clean and neatly dressed she was. She insisted though: "The weather is too bad, and you are too drunk. We will wait until morning to go."

Upon reaching the anchorage at Kittery Point, I was having some medical problems. The next morning we crossed the River to Portsmouth, New Hampshire where I received tests and treatment in the hospital emergency room.

We moored along the city dock which held only three to four boats. The tide and currents are very strong here. The next morning, the boat behind us, with an incoming tide, ran into our stern, touched the bow of the boat ahead of us, and then hit a piling, trying to leave the dockage. We plan our departure for slack water.

Boston, Massachusetts' inner harbor

Plays and concerts were presented throughout the summer in the park opposite our mooring. While there we saw "GREASE" in their outdoor theater.

Continuing south, our next stop was the city of Boston, one of the many cities who have renovated and restored their waterfront. *PRIME TIME* is tied up at Boston Inner Harbor, Constitution Marina in downtown Boston. We found many places to visit and things to see.

We toured the ship *"CONSTITUTION"*, the oldest commissioned Navy vessel still in service – we climbed Bunker Hill monument, 297 steps, 220 feet high – viewed the "Whites of Your Eyes" historical – followed the Red Line Freedom Trail to tour the city – the Paul Revere park and house – and the "Old Church" which had no pews, just wooded sectioned rooms with walls.

The Farmers' Market was very entertaining as we watched the merchants hawk their merchandise.

It was exciting to ride the subway for the first time. I feel the subway, several floors below the street, would be too spooky to use alone or after dark.

Three days later Ken reviews the tidal charts for the Cape Cod Canal. When we go through, it is still rough water and an incoming tide. After clearing the Canal, we head for Onset to lay over until the seas subside. Because Onset was over–flowing with boats, we continued on to Matapoissett on Buzzards Bay.

23

BUZZARDS BAY – HELL GATE

JULY 12– 13 – We didn't stop at New Bedford, separated from Fairhaven by the Acushnet River. This river opens directly into the ocean. We note interestingly on the chart, however, they have a mile long hurricane barrier coming in from each side of the river, which encloses all but 150 feet passage. If a major storm is forecasted, the gates close across the opening thus protecting the cities from the stormy seas.

NEWPORT – The American Cup race trials are on in Naragansett Bay in Newport. The harbors are completely full. We are on a mooring and take a shuttle water taxi the mile into shore. A mooring cost $15.00, normal cost was $5.00, and marina slips were $2.00 a foot.

The city has many historical places; we visited the oldest synagogue (1763) in America; the first Baptist church (1775) in America, and the St. Mary's church where J. F. Kennedy married Jackie in 1953.

Gorgeous, palatial homes surround the harbor. England's Prince Andrew is scheduled here for several days during which time several balls and festivities are planned.

Twelve miles up the Naragansett River is the small, unchanged harbor and town of Bristol. Local people do not want to improve the waterfront fearing .it might become another busy "Newport". They have several large industrial buildings and the PEARSON boat works.

Point Judith, harbor of refuge, is a very large area, separated from the ocean by a seawall. Once inside the bay, which was loaded with kelp, you feel you are right on the ocean. I said: "I am not comfortable about this anchorage". Because it was still early in the day, Ken said "let's continue on to Stonington". Our friend, the *FREEDOM*, was built in Stonington. Unfortunately, it was too late to go ashore to visit the many boatworks there.

There is now more boating activity, although we seem to be the only ones going south.

July 16 – We wind our way in the fog and haze through Fishers Sound and around several reefs to New London, Connecticut. Thunderstorms are forecasted. On shore, it is hot – 90 degrees and high humidity. The terrain is hilly , and with the steamy temperatures, bike riding was strenuous. But it did not stop us from enjoying New London's rich history.

We toured the beautiful and impressive grounds of the Coast Guard Academy – Union Station (1883), public library (1892) and the Antientest Burial Grounds (1653), oldest graveyard in New London. Also, the Nathan Hale School, a two story, 22x28 foot building built in 1775. Hale was schoolmaster there before entering the service.

Commercial fishermen were bringing in their catch. One had a large Mako shark.

Groton, Connecticut is just across the river and looks very commercial. Many submarines are supposed to be in the area but we have seen none so far.

July 18, 19, 20 – Duck Island Road, Northport and Manhasset Bay on Long Island Sound. All three days coming down the Sound were in haze and fog, visibility 2– 5 miles. At one point I worried an approaching freighter "was getting too close and would run over us". I never want to argue with a freighter, so after double checking our navigation, Ken said: "Just hold your course, the freighter will clear us. If you start changing course, it will only confuse him". Well, he did clear, but it was very close.

July 21 – Scenery and towns look different on our return trip. Perhaps it is because it is more relaxing and we have time to look around.

Many jets are seen taking off from LaGuardia airport. Helicopters and overhead cable cars transport people across the river to and from the airport.

24

HELL GATE – CAPE MAY

IT IS TIME again to check our tide tables to go through Hell Gate at slack water and proceed down the East River.

We see busy Manhattan, bumper to bumper traffic on the two four–lane highways, one of which is at water level under the buildings. Trees and shrubbery are planted on top of buildings and skyscrapers. Garbage is taken by scow barges to a dumping ground.

Governors Island is occupied by the United States Coast Guard who uses a ferry for transportation. There are also large ferries going to Staten Island for reportedly a ten–cent fare.

The Statute of Liberty, our Grand Lady, was impressively large and very beautiful. We sailed within a few feet of her.

We continue down New York Bay between Staten Island and Brooklyn, and return to New Jersey's Manasquan Inlet, the first major inlet off the ocean. The shore is lined with homes and many people on the beaches.

July 22 – Another wild and tiring day on the Atlantic Ocean between Manasquan Inlet and Atlantic City, seven and a half hours to go 50 miles. Northwest winds of 18–25 knots, gusts to 30, following seas 3 to 5 feet. Salt water spray covered the boat. Several times Ken would need to fill a tea kettle with our fresh water and cautiously climb onto the foredeck and wash the windshield so we could see.

The ocean and wind did not treat us kindly these 50 miles between the Inlet and Atlantic City. Going north took 11 hours and   returning south seven and a half. Ken jokingly said: "This is your favorite part of the cruise". It couldn't be farther from the truth.

July 22 We are at anchor at Atlantic City where the harbor is full of fishing boats. The wind never tapered enough to take our small dinghy to shore. This was all right, however, because as the day went by, we began to feel tired and were content to do nothing.

The next day, the winds tapered, the ocean calmed to its normal heaving motion – making for a very pleasant day. This will be our last Atlantic Ocean sailing for a while. It has been all "outside" from Cape May, New Jersey to Maine and back to Cape May. Visibility has been generally poor with much fog, haze and low clouds. We motored 90% of the time with little opportunity to use the sails.

Tomorrow we will be on more protected waters, going through the Cape May Canal.

25

CAPE MAY – NORFOLK, VIRGINIA

THE CITY OF Cape May has very quaint, many "gingerbread" homes, and numerous very old homes. The beach is lined with umbrellas, huts and hundreds of people. It cost $2.00 for a daily ticket to use the beach. We enjoyed walking the promenade along the ocean.

Fishermen bring in their catch to be weighed and recorded. This date one brought in an 8 foot, 125 lb. swordfish, and 12 foot, 675 lb. tiger shark, largest for the season. They said it took five men two hours to tire the shark and get it alongside. The shark got loose, however, and it took another three hours to get it in the boat, at which time they shot it three times in the head with a shotgun. The shark was so large it filled the aft deck. We were told tiger shark meat is not edible by humans.

July 25 – Travelling the length of the Delaware Bay, through the 12 mile long canal back into Chesapeake Bay, we dropped anchor in the Sassafras River.

July 26 – July and August on Chesapeake Bay is usually hot, hazy and little wind. We anchored in front of the U S Naval Academy in Annapolis.

At about 2330 hrs. sirens and emergency flashing lights awoke us from a sound sleep. One boat came through the harbor so fast, the wake just about threw me out of bed.

The commotion was due to a boating accident at the Chesapeake Bridge only a few miles away. A 30 ft. boat ran over a 17 ft. boat head–on, killing the three people on the smaller boat. Several Coast Guard boats and helicopters were bringing the bodies into the harbor to meet the ambulances.

July 27 – Oxford on the east side of the Bay is a very quaint place. We saw only two small general stores, 4 restaurants, and no gas stations.

Late in the day there is another boating accident at the Chesapeake Bay bridge. This time a yacht collided with a tug and barge. They were diving for people and debris.

We hear a steady creaking noise whenever you turn the wheel and believe it is in the steering linkage chain or cable. Fearing it might break and we would lose our steerage, Ken took the mechanism all apart, oiled and reassembled it. To do this, also required removing the compass, and calibrating it each time. We did this several times and it still creaked. And what was caused to be the problem? The nut securing the wheel was loose, and since tightening it up, the creak disappeared.

July 29 Leave for anchorage on Great Wimcomico River about 60 miles down the Bay. It turned out to be 70 miles, taking 11 hours. Winds were south, seas built 2–4 feet and very rough. Salt water sprayed over the boat, visibility very poor through salty windows. Wind is still strong in our protected anchorage.

The Bay has masses of jelly fish. By August they are so thick they can plug the inlets on your boat. Jelly Fish can inflict a painful sting if they come in contact with your body.

Report of two more men overboard in separate accidents, making four boating accidents in last two days on the Bay.

July 29 – We cross the Bay again to Fishing Bay at Deltonville, a very quaint fishing village. We primarily wanted to return to Taylors restaurant for their seafood buffet. It was again excellent. We rode our bikes there, however, they will come to the harbor and pick you up.

Weather forecast for tomorrow is not favorable for us – more Southwest winds, 15–20 m.p.h.. Winds like that rile up the Bay with short, choppy and sometimes high seas.

July 30 – The large James River flows into the Chesapeake on its way to the Atlantic Ocean. It separates Hampton Roads and Norfolk, Virginia. It is a very large area of water, heavy commercial traffic, with all channels well marked.

Norfolk, Virginia, is one of the largest seaports in the world. We picked our way through the congestion – in and around dozens of freighters and warships anchored in the Bay, and enormous shipyards with vessels in dry-dock. Some were from foreign countries. Some were extremely rusty and did not appear sea worthy. We felt pretty small in comparison to these very large vessels.

Weather had cleared by morning as we leave for an anchorage on Willoughby Bay, a short distance north of Norfolk. Upon entering the bay, we immediately discovered there was no room for us, nor did it look safe. We had to "jockey" back and forth in close quarters to get out of there and return to the busy, commercial waterway to Norfolk and start again on the Intercoastal Waterway.

26

BACK ON THE WATERWAY

AT NORFOLK, the Waterway starts again at Mile 0. From here it is 1243 statute miles to Key West.

The terrain and water are immediately different once you are on the ICW. It is a narrow channel with several low clearance bridges. The seas were calm and winds mild. It was only noon, so we decided to go a short way further to Great Bridge, Virginia.

Immediately north of Great Bridge, there is a lock and bridge coordinated to open on the hour. After a slight delay, we proceeded through and at 1415 we were secured to an outside wall.

Ken said: "It is great to be back in fresh water. I'm going to clean the boat." Standing on the wall, he cleaned one side. When we tried to turn the boat around to do the second side, the engine would not start. We were out of fuel.

The gauge showed one-eighth full but apparently was not accurate. We were thankful we didn't anchor in remote Willoughby Bay, or run out coming through the large commercial harbor at Norfolk.

Cyprus swamp along southern intercoastal waterway

27

GOING HOME

OUR PLAN WAS to leave the boat at the Atlantic Yacht Basin in fresh water and go home for a couple months to let our families know we were still alive and doing well.

We needed a car. There were no rentals or bus service here. Another boater who was leaving his boat temporarily, had a car and was leaving for New Jersey. We accepted his offer of a ride to Norfolk.

On a very hot Saturday afternoon, we covered used car lots and purchased an "As is" 1978 Olds Cutlass station wagon. This car was our "character car", as each day it would have a different noise or problem, ranging from the speedometer cable, air conditioner out of order, no compression or "get up and go", and the upholstery which we fastened with paper clips and safety pins, kept falling down over the driver's head.

We packed the car, tied on the bicycles, and excitedly headed for home.

BACK HOME – July 30 – November 1 – What fun it was to see family and friends. We stayed in my mother's home where our furniture was stored.

While riding our bikes around the city on a Sunday afternoon, we see a darling house for sale. Surprisingly Ken said: "Why don't you call the salesman?" I thought: "Should I call and waste his time?"

I knew our cruising was not over. Yet I also knew that as soon as my feet were back on home soil, I wanted to start looking for another house. "Well, it wouldn't hurt to

151

look", I told myself, "and get a feel of the real estate market".

So I called the salesman – he came over to show the house – and within a few days we bought it.

Three extremely busy weeks remained before returning to Great Bridge. We moved in during this time, had new carpeting installed, $1700 electrical work, new appliances and cupboards. Ken added attic insulation, and I wallpapered one bath.

November 1 – We locked up the house, said "good-bye" to our family and friends. In our trusty "As Is" car, we returned to Great Bridge to get aboard our *PRIME TIME*. The car was put in storage, and we started our return trip to Florida via the Intercoastal Waterway.

28

BACK ON THE WATERWAY
RETURN TO MARATHON

WE MOVE practically every day with our main goal to back-track to Fort Myers, Florida. The following were our anchorages (unless specified as a marina):

Mile 50 Coinjock
Mile 102 Albermarle Sound and Alligator River
Mile 187 Adams Creek
Mile 244 On ICW after Albermarle Sound, Pamlico Sound and Neuse River, to Hammock Bay south of Morehead City.

Mile 283 Wrightsville Beach (marina)
Mile 344 Little River, South Carolina
Mile 423 Georgetown
Mile 487 Stono River

Mile 533 Beaufort, South Carolina
Mile 583 Thunderbolt marina (marina)
Mile 623 Johnson Creek
Mile 695 Cumberland Island

TRANSMISSION PROBLEMS – November 15 – On our way to a planned anchorage mile 735, we stopped for fuel at Fernandina, mile 717. At mile 750, on a routine check of the bilge, we noticed oil floating on top of the water. A closer inspection showed oil coming out of the transmission vent. Ken said: "This can mean only one thing – the transmission oil cooler". Due to electrolysis, the interior of the cooler had deteriorated causing salt water to mix with the oil.

We immediately went to the side of the channel and dropped the anchor to analyze our problem. Should we call the marina at Fernandina Beach? Meanwhile, a 22 foot outboard came by and offered help. He towed *PRIME TIME* the three miles back to Jacksonville Beach Marina. After a new part was put on the transmission, it was flushed several times to get the salt water out. It appeared no harm had been done. Luckily we noticed the problem in time. Repairs cost $138.81 and we had no further problems with the transmission.

November 17 Mile 765 – north of Vedra Beach. It is a full moon, clear and COLD at night. Just to be on the safe side, Ken pumped and flushed the transmission again.

Mile 829 Daytona Beach
Mile 847 New Smyrna Beach
Mile 909 Merritt Island
Mile 982 North of St. Lucie Inlet
Mile 1025 West Palm Beach.

November 24 Mile 1078 – Maule Lake. HAPPY THANKSGIVING. We had pork chops for dinner while anchored in a small bay with other boats. Mid afternoon the weather took a sudden turn for the worse – tornado water spouts came through, spun us 360 degrees. Other boats' anchors broke loose and they were floating free.

Mile 1084 Monty Trainer Marina at Dinner Key.
Mile 1147 Rodriguez Key in Hawk Channel. It took an hour to set two anchors in the coral bottom. The northeast wind and being exposed to the ocean, made the seas rough in the anchorage. It was about half way to Marathon from Miami, and little chance of finding a better place. There was no choice but to stay here overnight.
Mile 1194 Fara Blanca, Marathon

29

MARATHON TO FORT MYERS

DECEMBER 3 – It is a good day's run to Everglades anchorage from Marathon and we wanted an early start. The southern sky appeared so very threatening, I was hesitant about leaving.

After an hour so, Ken said: "We have just got to go. Those clouds will not do anything." Quickly we prepared to leave. No wind to sail, we motored at seven plus knots all the way. He set the anchor just as the sun was disappearing over the horizon. We have noticed that, especially in Florida, that when the sun goes down, there is no lengthy sunset. In a few minutes, it is very dark.

The morning's dark clouds, or storm? The clouds dissipated and there was no storm.

Heavy fog rolls in our anchorage at Fort Myers Beach. Ken, after starting the engine, checked over the side to make sure the water pump was working. He said: "My God, there is an oil slick on the water. It is oil mixed with water coming out of the exhaust." The only possible cause of something like this he said would be the engine motor oil cooler deteriorating and causing a leak. He immediately shut the engine off to prevent any more oil being lost.

Ken boarded the dinghy, and in the fog, went to shore for a new motor oil cooler. Several days earlier when the transmission oil cooler was replaced, he was told that because both coolers were of the same age, it was very possible that the engine motor oil cooler would also need to be replaced soon. The repairman was right. Fortunately, in both instances, we were near an area where we could get repairs.

We arrive at Fort Myers Yacht Basin and plan to stay until mid March.

30

FORT MYERS TO THE BAHAMAS

MARCH 16 – After another great "winter" at Fort Myers, *PRIME TIME* leaves to rendezvous with the *GRAY-BOB* at Fort Myers Beach. *GRAY-BOB* had his anchor down and all ready for us to tie alongside. Under a big beautiful full moon, together we made plans for the next few days – anchorages again at Everglade City, Marathon and Rodriguez Key. We had three beautiful days on anchor.

Early morning weather looked favorable. The wind was out of the east. Hawks Channel was choppy. As the day went by, the wind got stronger, and the seas inside the reef turbulent. The Atlantic Ocean outside the reef must have been quite wild.

Making the turn into Biscayne Channel, we had a very strong following sea. My arms ached from trying to keep between the buoys.

On March 24th, we anchored in Hurricane Harbor. We are studying our Bahama charts more seriously now. We plan to leave from Hurricane Harbor as soon as the weather improves. In the meantime, because of the delay in departure, we make several trips back and forth to Miami Dinner Key to replenish provisions and to Belchers on Government Cut for fuel.

At Dinner Key a young couple planned to be married on a chartered cruiser. The wedding party was there, the photographer, several musicians, boxes of fresh flowers, caterer with food for thirty-five guests, but the chartered boat was not. *GRAY-BOB,* after making several

159

calls, located the cruiser several miles up the Miami River in dry dock. The couple hired another boat, and finally got out on Biscayne Bay for their wedding and reception.

31

BAHAMA ISLANDS

THE BAHAMAS were discovered by Christopher Columbus in 1492. The closest cay (pronounced key) lies approximately 50 miles from Florida's coastline. These cays form a 700 mile–long archipelago of islands, cays and reefs. Most of the cays are uninhabited. Generally, it is the crystal clear water, mauve to pale blues and greens, and the dazzling white beaches that attract the boater.

All vessels must clear with Customs and Immigration at the nearest point of entry.

Cruising the Bahamas is different than in the United States. Most of the cruising is done by "sketch" charts. There are few markers or beacons and only a few lighthouses. There are many shoals and coral heads. Navigating by bearings, sometimes multiple, is usually necessary. In many places, piloting is done entirely by eye – color of the water indicating the depth. It is strongly recommended you do not sail at night.

The Gulf Stream's current can be six knots, but most usually is approximately two and a half knots. It is imperative you correct your course accordingly. The Stream, more than 1500 feet deep, is a warm oceanic current emanating from the Gulf of Mexico. It flows northward along the eastern coast, and then northeasterly towards the British Isles.

BAHAMAS

32

LEAVE FOR THE BAHAMAS
ABACOS

ON APRIL 7th, the weather finally cleared. We leave our Hurricane Harbor anchorage at 0450 (before dawn) and work our way through the darkness out of the channel.

Our two captains, *PRIME TIME* and *GRAY-BOB* had computed the Gulf Stream current and set the LORANS for a landfall at Cat Cay. It was exciting to cross the Gulf Stream. The cobalt blue water looks like a separate river flowing northward in the ocean.

As soon as we were in Bahama waters, we hoisted our yellow (quarantine) flag until we cleared customs at Cat Cay. After clearance, we removed the yellow, and as a courtesy, flew the Bahama flag below our starboard spreader. Guns are also registered when you check in at customs.

The next morning we depart early (0530) to cover the 75 nautical miles across the Great Bahama Bank for Chub Cay. Depth of water crossing the Bank is nine to twenty feet, with some shoaling areas dry at low tide.

At 0825 *GRAY-BOB* radioed that his engine was overheating.   The impeller in the water pump had disintegrated and, therefore, was not pumping sea water to his engine. We dropped our anchors in this shallow water while he made repairs with spare parts carried for such emergencies. At 0950 we were on our way again. This will

163

make our anticipated eleven hour run longer now. There is no place to stop along the way on these shallow banks so we continue on to Chub Cay.

Graydon and Bobbie Klopp, captain and first mate of GRAY-BOB

GRAY–BOB crossing the Gulf Stream enroute to Bahamas

At 2000 in total darkness, we weave in and around numerous boats at anchor outside Chub Cay's entrance. We had no choice but to anchor in this crowded area. Total time out for the day was 14 1/2 hours.

By this time the wind was whistling. The seas became rough. We were in a protected area but due to a substantial surge we were rocking sideways in the wave troughs. This lasted all through the night.

After a restless night, in the morning we moved into the marina taking the last slip available. Cost was $24.50 a day, plus $18.00 for electricity, 30 cents a gallon for water.

The day was exciting:

1. Just outside the harbor, a fishing boat, a 38 ft. Hatteras, broke a fuel line and exploded. The Bahamian Defense Force towed it in and pumped it out. The only person on board escaped by dinghy to shore. The boat was a mess.

2. We visited the crew on the Defense Force boat. All young Bahamian boys.

3. A fish tournament for "billed fish" was going on. Five boats brought in six fish. The weighing–in station had a reception (bar set up and native music) for the return of the catch.

4. We walked to the beach, on a path of pine trees forming a canapy to the ocean breakers and black coral rock.

5. Bobbie and I went swimming in a pool the club allows mariners to use.

6. During the very hard rain storm in the evening, we put out buckets to collect the fresh water.

(Fresh water is very scarce and expensive. Homes collect rain water and store in underground cisterns.)

7. The next morning as we prepare to leave for Nassau, we hear on the radio that a plane crashed on Chub Cay at 0400. It had a load of cocaine. No one was found aboard. Pilot was missing.

8. Later we hear another report that two more planes went down on Chub Cay. Again, they, too, were loaded with coke, no pilots nor crew was found.

The Bahama's weather is similar to Florida's. The report today is that two tornadoes hit Florida and a truck was blown off the Skyway Bridge. Weather here is unsettled but no storms are expected.

NEW PROVIDENCE ISLAND. Nassau, population over 100,000, is the capital city of New Providence Island. The island is 21 miles long and seven miles wide and is the most important, economically and socially, of all the inhabited islands of the Bahamas.

The entrance to the harbor is well buoyed. Because it has a depth of 36 feet, it can accommodate the largest of cruise ships.

All vessels, pleasure craft included, must clear with Nassau Harbor Control when coming in or leaving the harbor.

In the harbor, tide on the flood can reach a velocity of two and a half knots.

After a five and a quarter hour sail in these beautiful waters, we arrived at Nassau.

While on the boat, air temperature was cool and comfortable. On shore, however, it was very hot. We walked two miles to town to visit the Straw Market, where Bobbie and I bought much needed sun hats. Then we couldn't resist having ice cream at Howard Johnsons.

Nassau's boatyard. Many boats looked beyond repair or sunken.

Fresh water supply is rain water collected from roofs and stored in cisterns

Rather than walk in the heat, we took the "jitney" back to the boat. What a thrill that was. The driver fortunately missed the walls as we careened down along the narrow, winding roads.

The next day we took a fascinating and informative bus tour. This ride was more relaxing than in the jitney.

BAHAMA CUISINE – In many areas, restaurants feature only Bahamian cooking. Bahamian cuisine is spicier than American food, and is more fish than meat. Their national dishes are Conch (pronounced Conk) and Peas and Rice. They also have very good bread but it has no preservatives.

A mollusk, the Conch live in a large shell. Bahamian divers leave the shells on shore after extracting the Conch. The reason being they don't want to dive for empty shells. Bahamians eat the meat raw the same as Americans eat raw oysters and clams, believing they increase their virility.

Peas and Rice, like grits in our southern states, is served whether you want it or not. It is prepared with tomato paste and salt pork, and if you like, they add hot peppers.

We had lunch in a Native Bahamian restaurant. I had steamed Turtle, Peas and Rice (without the hot peppers). Ken, Graydon and Bobbie had Conch salad. They liked the Conch but thought it a little tough to chew.

Fishermen use a concave shell as a horn by blowing into it. Graydon bought one of these shells. We kidded him that he sounded like a bull moose in his attempts to make a sound.

33

EXUMA ISLANDS

ON APRIL 12th we leave at 0915 for ALLAN'S CAY, 34 miles from Nassau. It is a rather spooky day, going over the shallow banks and many coral heads appearing as dark masses under the surface. Our LORANS are not giving good accurate information. There are no lighthouses, buoys or markers to tell one island from another. But we made a safe landfall at 1550.

Within minutes after dropping anchor, we are in the dinghy and heading for shore. The seashore was covered with dead coral making walking tricky.

Many Iguana lizards, some a couple feet long, almost camouflaged by the rocks, were sunning themselves.

HAWKSBILL – WARDWICK WELLS – Another beautiful day greets us this morning. We could be tempted to stay at Allen's Cay but we go on to uninhabited Hawksbill Cay. This beautiful cay was found to be an area open to the sea and possibly uncomfortable for the night so we went on to Wardwick Wells Cay, another 20 miles.

WARDWICK WELLS is difficult to get into because it is surrounded by shifting banks. Much care should be exercised in locating the channel. Once inside the anchorage, it is recommended you use two anchors.

Bobbie and Dorothy returning from the beach. A very narrow channel with sufficient water for boat navigating

*Graydon, Bobbie and Dorothy at Wardwick Wells –
supposedly a haunted cay*

A large hollow rock, Thunderball Cave, named after James Bond movie

PRIME TIME and GRAY–BOB lashed together

Ken grilling our supper off the stern of PRIME TIME

Graydon cracking the shell to remove the Conch

Navigational aid (a stick marking the channel) as we approached Spanish Wells

We learned later we did not enter through the recommended channel. Fortunately, we had sufficient water and avoided the rocks and coral.

We walked to the highest point where people had built a rock pile and stuck in it a long pole (to conquer the hill). They left messages in bottles and names on boards to signify their being there.

Wardwick Wells is supposedly a haunted cay. On a full moon night, you might hear voices talking with each other or singing hymns. This was a full moon night, but we heard nothing.

Today, April 16, is a very rainy, and unusually cloudy day. To save our fresh water supply, we break out the buckets and pails to collect the rain water.

STANIEL CAY'S anchorage is shallow and has been brushed clean by the current. It took almost an hour to set the anchors in the rocky and coral bottom. We finally settled in 5 feet of water at low tide. (We were actually sitting on the bottom)

Staniel Cay is less than one square mile in area and only 60 people. They have a yacht club and one Inn called "Happy Peoples". The seats of the chairs in the Inn are covered with large yellow "Happy People" faces. I asked: "What is the significance of the name, 'Happy People'?" and their reply was: "We are just happy people."

They sell water for 15 cents a gallon so we filled our tanks.

The Dive Shop told us of a cave to snorkel in at low tide. This is a very large room-size rock, practically hollow inside with openings to the sky. It is filled with live coral and fish. These fish will take and eat chunks of bread from your hand.

This rock, called "Thunderball Cave", is named after the James Bond (Sean Connery) movie filmed in the cavernous sea garden. They have come back to use it again for segments in "Never Say Never Again".

Near the anchorage, there were many fish and a great variety of coral. Ken dived for several sand dollars and a Conch shell which had a live crab in it. He also saw a lobster hiding behind the rocks. Unfortunately, lobsters were "out of season" during our visit here.

Staniel Cay is such a beautiful cay, we can see why people return to it.

GEORGE TOWN – After a very pleasant stay at Little Farmers Cay, we prepare to leave for George Town.

As we cross Galliot Cut, there is very strong tide running against us. We poured on the power and plowed through the three to four seas just off our bow. The wind is now howling and seems to be getting stronger and more unstable.

Seven hours later, two hours longer than it should have been, we reached our anchorage. This anchorage off Stocking Island across the bay from George Town is quiet and frequented by many boats.

In the morning, the wind has tapered enough to take the dinghy across the channel to George Town.

George Town, population 800, is a charming community. It is cruising headquarters for the most southern part of the Bahamas. You can purchase most supplies. It also has air connections daily to south Florida and Nassau.

Downtown is a couple repair shops, fishing tackle, gift, and a straw market.

The Club Peace and Plenty hotel and dining room on the waterfront now serves American/Bahamian food. Its legend is it was originally a slave market, then a sponge warehouse, and finally a hostelry.

There is one tiny Baptist church. The Anglican black church was high on a hill overlooking the area in all directions. We went inside and saw a very quaint, old wooden church. The Stations of the Cross were all hand carved plaques. Tomorrow is Easter Sunday but there were no flowers in the church.

Ken, Graydon and Bobbie enjoyed snorkeling in the surf. I said: "It is too rough for me" so I played in shallow water.

We see a fantastic bright "blue hole", a bottomless hole that goes directly down and out to the ocean. The hole is affected by the tide. Divers are warned not to dive near there to avoid being drawn down into the current.

It is April 22, Easter Sunday and another gorgeous day. I am getting better at snorkeling, or is it because today the water is calm I had less difficulty keeping water out of the tube.

Daughter and son-in-law, Marla and Barry Boone, arrive to spend a week aboard the *PRIME TIME*. We picked them up at the George Town fuel dock. Wind was strong and current was running at the dock. We filled with fuel, purchased water at ten cents a gallon, and returned to Elizabeth Harbor anchorage. Again we lashed alongside the *GRAY-BOB*.

We went snorkeling at three different coves. At one, the water was again too rough for me so I didn't get out to the reef. The men tried their Bahama Hawaiian slings again.

Returning to Staniel Cay, we finally have a nice wind for sailing. Up go the jib and mizzen. But shortly the winds were too much for that amount of sail, so we reefed the jib.

I am still trying to catch a fish. Now I have two lines trailing off the stern. *GRAY-BOB* caught another – a nice Spanish mackerel – – my hooks are still bare.

We returned to the mouth of the Sound. It was rough and the tide running. We saw many fish, a two foot barracuda, and a dead five foot shark. The fellows tried to spear the barracuda but he was too foxy for them. We were uneasy about our dinghies being swept out to sea so decided to return to our boats.

Barry and Marla were in *PRIME TIME's* dinghy. Shortly, the recoil for the starter cord broke, and they couldn't start the motor. They tried to use the oars. Struggling against the tide and making no headway, the *GRAY-BOB* secured a tow line to them. At one point we

181

actually stood still making no progress against the running tide. We inched ourselves forward and eventually made it safely back to the boats.

I sat alone in the cockpit (the others had gone to bed) and watched the lightening in the distance. It rained some during the night.

I have the post cards yet I wrote in Georgetown two days ago. Perhaps I can mail them here at Staniel Cay. I am told mail goes out every Sunday by boat and will take a week to reach the States.

We tour Staniel Cay again with Barry and Marla. They want to treat us to dinner at "Happy Peoples".

At "Happy Peoples", you need to make a reservation several hours ahead and place your order at that time. They offer two or three selections. They serve only once – at 1900.

Marla and Barry went in *PRIME TIME*'S dinghy and we went with *GRAY-BOB*. It was very dark returning in the dinghies to our boats using only flashlights for light.

HIGHBORNE CAY – our last stop in the Exumas. – We reach Highborne Cay at 1320 with plenty of time to go swimming. However, we saw two sharks around our boats which convinced us that we would not be swimming here today. Several large fishing boats had brought in their catch. A few men were at the end of the pier cleaning their fish and throwing the innards overboard, thus attracting the sharks and seagulls. We enjoyed the especially pretty scenery from the decks of our boats.

GOOD BYE TO THE EXUMAS. We go to Eleuthera Island tomorrow.

34

ELEUTHERA ISLAND

ELEUTHERA ISLAND is considered one of the most beautiful of the Bahama Islands. It is about ninety miles long by two to three miles wide. The terrain is rolling hills, trees and lakes. Portions of the coast are high steep cliffs.

The island is mainly agricultural. At one time they shipped hundreds of tons of pineapple each year to America and England. They no longer do this, but they still supply Nassau with tomatoes, corn, citrus and pineapple. In addition, they have cattle and dairy industry, plus many deluxe resorts.

ROCK SOUND – The channel to our anticipated anchorage was shallow and full of rocks. The wind was against the tide, causing rough seas on our bow. We would plunge in and out – spray covering the boat. As we got in more protected water and away from the outlet, the seas subsided making for more comfortable sailing.

There is another "Blue Hole" called "Ocean Blue Hole". Like the other one, it is a deep blue, land locked hole leading to the ocean.

We enjoyed the quaint village and talking to the natives. The buildings, fences and walls are all painted the same pastel color as the house.

Cars drive on the left side of the road which appear too narrow for two cars to pass. Many people just drive down the middle. There are no sidewalks. Pedestrians need to carefully watch for cars coming from either direction.

Typical narrow streets, abundant flowers, many dogs

GOVERNOR'S HARBOR – Governor's Harbor is one of the few cays which has adequate facilities. They have food stores, doctor and dentist, a bank and post office. All government offices are painted pink.

Today the post office is closed and I still have my mail written several days ago. There are no drop boxes on the streets. We asked the police station to take it with their mail – they would not do this. We inquired of a gift shop merchant. He said: "I will take the mail to the post office Monday only if we would not sue him if the mail didn't reach its destination." We assured him we would not do this and left our mail (postcards) with him.

We visit a fisherman's shack and I ask: "What lures will catch fish in these waters?" He sold me an 8" long lure, "guaranteed to catch fish". I bought another lure from the market. Now I should catch something.

Well, I did, but it was adding insult to injury. Bobbie was reeling in a 31" barracuda. At the same time, using my new lure purchased from the market, my reel started spinning. I thought "finally". But what I had on my hook was an eight inch snake fish.

Barry and Marla's vacation is coming to an end. They need to return to their jobs in Michigan. Here at Governor's Harbor, he tried to get a commuter plane to take them to Nassau where they had reservations for a flight to the states. He paid $30.00 taxi fare to the Governor's Harbor airport eight miles away, only to learn arrangements for a flight had to be made downtown. The nine passenger plane's pilot is in his early 20's. Barry is not comfortable flying with him over all the open water, but he had no other choice but to hire him.

The sounds of the village drift over the water to our anchorage. In the evening, the rhythms of a loud steel drum band blared out across the water. They played until the wee hours of the morning. Its psychedelic lights cast a colorful glow. There are many roosters on the island. They all start crowing at the break of dawn. Quite a serenade.

185

In the morning, April 29, we say "good-bye" to Barry and Marla as they leave for the airport to catch their little commuter plane to go to Nassau.

In the meantime, we prepare for our next anticipated stop, Spanish Wells. On the way, I again put out the lines over the stern. On one, I put my new lure. I said: "I am going to give it just one hour, and if no fish by then, I'll change again."

Within minutes, my pole started jumping and the line was spinning out. What excitement. As I was reeling it in, I could see it was a large fish. And it was. A 33 inch barracuda weighing seven to eight pounds.

Just as Ken got it in the net, Barry and Marla"s little plane flew over. We held the fish up hoping they would see it. Then Ken carefully took the fish out of the net, avoiding its large sharp teeth and put it back into the sea.

CURRENT CUT – Continuing on to Spanish Wells, we approach the Current Cut channel. This channel is only about 150 feet across. At times the tide can run at ten knots. On our port, the sea was breaking over the rocks. To our starboard was a swift current.

Our concern was to stay away from the rocks and stay closer to starboard in hopefully deeper water.

Ken took the wheel and as he started to power through the current, *PRIME TIME* hit a shallow spot and went hard aground.

We hoisted a sail hoping the wind would heel us over far enough to get the keel off the bottom. That didn't help. The tide was rising. The simplest alternative was to wait for the tide to come in. In the meantime, Graydon and Bobbie came over in their dinghy and took our anchor, set it out fifty feet. Shortly thereafter, Ken kedged us off with the engine's assist.

I finally caught a fish − 31" barracuda

We were delayed one hour and fifteen minutes. By now it is too late in the day to go the distance to Spanish Wells. We headed instead for Royal Island and reached there at 1845.

ROYAL ISLAND Island, which is a private island, has a beautiful anchorage area where we spent the night. From our anchorage, we could see only a few houses, mostly in disrepair and seemingly abandoned. Several posted signs on the banks read: "Do Not Trespass" and "If you come ashore, you will be shot". Needless to say, we stayed aboard our boats.

In front of one home was a stone breakwater with a dock. At this dock was a large open runabout boat with twin outboards.

Tonight for supper we have chop suey and a small amount of barracuda. Barracuda is not one of our favorite food fishes. Plus you are discouraged from eating large barracuda due to mineral contaminates .

Water from Royal Island to Spanish Wells is shallow – five and a half to ten feet. This morning the wind is strong and clouds threatening. It looks like a storm coming in. I think to myself: "I am concerned the wind will push us out of the narrow channel." Channels here are marked by small poles in the water, not the standard buoys we are accustomed to in the states.

Our captains said they "would prefer to have more sunshine to determine depth of water but there is really no reason to wait."

After lunch the anchors are pulled and we leave for Spanish Wells. Shortly it is obvious we are in shallow water. There was just enough depth to keep us from touching bottom, but we did kick up sand for one–third mile. It was a short one and a half hours to reach Spanish Wells.

SPANISH WELLS is one of the prettiest villages in the Bahamas. Its name comes the Spaniards' visits many years ago. They thought its well water was the sweetest in all of the Bahamas.

The sources of income for the island's inhabitants are fishing and some agriculture – tomatoes, vegetables, bananas and citrus.

It is another quaint village. Homes are very small and painted light colors. Streets are very narrow, enough room for one car. Many people use Honda bikes. Sidewalks are also narrow and in disrepair.

We bought a seven and a half pound Grouper from a fisherman. The fellows kneeled precariously on the swim ladder to clean the fish. They found this task quite challenging but well worth the effort – the grouper was excellent eating.

That night about 2100 darkness had just set in. There was a rather large twin–engine plane circling the harbor and village at a very low altitude. The fourth time around the engine started to sputter as though he were having engine problems. I said to Ken: "I think the pilot is looking for a place to unload his "pot".

A few minutes later Ken said: "There it is. It has crashed." The cars on shore had focused their lights on the plane so you could see it in the darkness. The plane crashed one–fifth mile from us, nosed into the coral.

Several boats had reached the scene within minutes of the crash. We elected not to go out by boat but to observe what we could from our deck and investigate in the morning.

The next morning at 0900 we went over to the crash scene. The plane was a DC–3 originally used in World War two as a transport and later used by the airlines. Three young fellows were busily stripping the plane of its instruments and anything else of value. There were only a few instruments and speakers for them to take. The pilot and co–pilot seats were in very worn condition. The passenger compartment was completely stripped, right down to the plane's shell, thus accommodating a large cargo. The side door was off. Floating nearby was a large auxiliary fuel tank carried to extend their flight hours. It had been attached to the exterior of the airplane.

189

These young fellows told us the crew had vanished prior to anyone from the village getting out to the airplane last night. Apparently at least one of the crew persons was injured because they said there was a substantial amount of blood in the cockpit when they got there. By morning the tide has washed it all away.

These drug runners by pre–arrangement, drop their load elsewhere before ditching the airplane. This crew was picked up by their buddies prior to anyone reaching the scene. This, again, is according to the young fellows stripping the airplane.

While we were there, the Bahamas Air Sea Rescue Association (BASRA) arrived from Nassau. They were there only minutes, appeared to make a written report and then left. Was this all they were going to do? Was this considered just another drug drop? We wondered.

We scout further around the island and find another abandoned plane ditched and now on the beach. This one happened last August. This plane, too, was completely stripped.

The channel between Spanish Wells at the northern tip of the Eleuthera Island and the Abacos can be quite hazardous. Due to the reefs, it is recommended that you have a local pilot take you through.

We decided to go back to the Royal Island harbor for one night. In the morning we would proceed up the Atlantic side to the Abacos.

Back at Royal Island, we were playing cards under the lights of our lanterns. It was about an hour after sunset (total darkness). Suddenly we heard a boat with no lights roar by us on his way out of the harbor. This boat had to come from the private dock mentioned earlier. Putting two and two together, it was not difficult to figure out what was going on and realize why they were so adamant about anyone coming ashore on their land.

At this point, we became uneasy, realizing we were witnessing a drug operation. We doused our lights, got our guns ready and sat in the darkness. The outboard never returned that night. It was a restless night.

Morning came and it was another beautiful sunny, warm day in the Bahamas. We hoisted the anchors at 0630 and headed for Little Harbor in the Abacos.

Drug plane comes to rest after dropping its cargo offshore

191

35

THE ABACOS

THE ABACO'S water and beaches are beautiful. Many
people consider them   exceeded only by the Exumas,
possibly the world's best.   It is the second largest (650
square miles) cay in the chain of islands. Elevation – 120
feet.

The Bight of Abaco (the area on the west side of the
island) is shallow and frequented very little. Cruising is
preferred on the east side where there are several cays
providing popular stops for the boater.

LITTLE HARBOR – Our cruise from Royal Harbor to
Little Harbor was 65–70 miles on the Atlantic Ocean. The
ocean was lumpy with four foot seas on our aft quarter. As
we neared our anchorage, and getting in shallow water, it
was difficult distinguishing between the breakers' white
water (aptly called the Boilers), and the white caps of the
ocean.   My arms and shoulders tensed from steering
through this uncomfortable area.

The next morning, May 3, we moved two miles
closer to Little Harbor. Where we anchored there was a
surge and very sloppy. We would make a decision about
staying here after a visit to the island.

We visited world renown Randolph Johnston's art
gallery of   sculptors made of bronze and wood.   His
hospitality included a tour of his work shop. His retail
department had some earrings listed at $2,000. Mrs.

193

Johnston and their son, Pete, and daughter–in–law are also sculptors in their own right.

Petes Pub, about 12 x 18 feet, and seats about ten people, is open only a couple hours after the studio closes. Pete sounds a Conch shell horn to let you know it is open. This Pub is the former pilot and deck house of the Johnston's 50 foot schooner.

We followed the trail to an abandoned light house on the ocean side. There isn't much left there except a fantastic view of the wild breakers crashing over the rocks.

Ken, Graydon and Bobbie explored one of the caves. They carefully climbed over the coral rocks to reach its entrance. Inside there are many small bats and hermit crabs. Do you wonder why I didn't want to go too?

The surge was still too much for the two boats being tied together. We separated and set out to search for better water, finally returning to our anchorage of the night before.

MARSH HARBOR – Continuing north, we reach Marsh Harbor where you will find most anything you might need. It has a bank, hardware store, drug store, post office, supermarket, laundry and airport.

In very hot temperature, and no shade, we walk the half–mile for groceries. Later, Bobbie and I enjoyed the marina's pool even though the water was very dirty. At least it cooled us off. You need to get your chores done in the morning as the afternoon sun is almost unbearable.

A sign over the marina walkway read: "Laundry, $6.00 a load." I didn't hesitate to gather up enough for two loads. When the laundry was finished, the ladies said: "That will be $18.00". I replied: "How come $18.00? I only had two loads." She answered: "We thought some of it needed bleach." After all these days doing it the rub–a–dub–dub method, my laundry did look dingy. It now looked good again and I appreciated their special attention given to it.

We purchased bananas and tomatoes from the native ladies who carry their produce in baskets resting on their heads. They didn't seem to understand English very well.

194

They might be Haitians as the Bahamians all speak fluent English.

Ken purchased from the market a grouper large enough for a couple meals. Later in the day, a fishing boat captain gave us a four meal supply of fresh dolphin (not Flipper).

It was interesting listening to Bahama radio news, especially regarding death notices. Because most transportation was by boat, and mail came by boat no more than once a week, it was speedier to give information by radio. A regular program consisted of reading complete obituaries, lists of survivors, plus funeral arrangements.

After several attempts, I finally reached my sister, Betty, by telephone. Thankfully, she had no bad news to relay. I became choked up talking with her. Guess I am a bit ready for going home.

GRAY-BOB's son has arrived to cruise with them for several days. They leave to visit some of the other cays. We go on to Hope Town and will rendezvous with them there.

HOPE TOWN – *PRIME TIME* is with *GRAY-BOB* again, We tour Hope Town, one of the most scenic and visited places in the Abacos. Its population is only about 300 but it has all the necessities and amenities of a larger village.

The highlight of our visit was climbing up the red and white candy stripe lighthouse. This structure, 120 feet above sea level, is still lighted by kerosene. The keeper climbs the one-hundred spiral steps and uses a match to ignite the fuel.

Two families, living on either side of the lighthouse, work the two shifts (1800–2400 and 2400 to 0600).

Every 2 hours the keeper needs to climb the one-hundred steps, hand pump the two air tanks, and hand wind the pulleys, much like winding a clock. Occasionally the light goes out, necessitating him to make another trip to re-light it.

The one housekeeper's two children ran down to the dock to help us secure the dinghy. They expect some payment for this. Bobbie gave one a quarter. The youngster said, "What can I get with this?" She replied: "You can return it if you don't want it." He kept it.

MAN–O–WAR – The channel coming in to Man––War is extremely shallow. We bounced for a mile in 5 feet of water. Not a secure feeling.

Man–O–War is immaculate. You see very few vehicles. Major type of transportation is the motor bike, and they are everywhere.

Houses are freshly painted. Hundreds of flowers in bloom were in their yards and window planters. They have a Methodist and a Pentacostal church. Many people have religious sayings painted on their homes.

People are very kind and cordial. I visited with one lady who was sitting in her house, just inside the open door. She had an artificial arm and hand, but with her "clamp", she was crocheting blouses and dresses for resale at Marsh Harbor. It took her a day and a half to do a blouse and was paid $40. She has trained 54 other native ladies to do this.

The beauty shop was a lady working on her front porch. She was giving a permanent to one of her several customers.

They sell no liquor in restaurants, bars or package stores.

We ordered dinner at Dock 'N Dine and ate at a outdoor picnic table. The fried grouper was delicious.

The little one–room school house was in session. Windows and doors were open – no glass or screens.

A ten by ten foot building had three doors in the front, one leading to the post office, another for radio-communication, and the other for the police.

The cemetery was on a bank over–looking the ocean. Most graves were old and neglected. Many had wooden posts for a marker which had deteriorated to a small stump. Few graves had flowers. We were told it takes six days for a Haitian man to dig a grave in the limestone. There were three open graves already dug for future use.

This cay is the Bahamas ship building center for wooden boats. They use some power tools, but much of the

196

work is done by hand. They search for trees having the "bend" they want. You still see some of their fifty–year old boats in these waters.

The Sail Shop has several people sewing all kinds of hats, bags, anything you want out of canvas.

The pace is slow at Man––War. Many of the little shops are open a few hours of the day or perhaps not at all.

GREAT GUANA – A short hop today of twelve to fourteen miles to another beautiful anchorage just off the beach.

Ken thought this would be a good time to clean the bottom of the boat. He hung on with a suction cup attached to the side with one hand, and scrubbed with the other. I swam around keeping an eye on him – and for sharks. It was a strenuous day for him.

The wind is quite strong, but not steady. It feels like a storm is on its way. Our captains   decide if the wind comes up or seas build, it would be wise to separate the boats.

Great Guana is one of our favorite places. It is most beautiful with several outstanding beaches. (We have learned since that they have dredged the harbor and small cruise ships anchor off shore.)

We decided to stay another day rather than go to Manjack and then back to Marsh Harbor for Graydon's son and daughter–in–law to catch their plane.

We leave Great Guana and return to Marsh Harbor.

On the way, and again trolling, my line started running out, the reel was spinning. From the tug on the line, I was sure it was a big one. Well, it could have been at one time. When I finally got it to the stern, all I could see was a piece of fish. Apparently a larger fish took it for bait, chopped it off right behind the gills.   All I had on my hook was the head and gills of a good size Spanish Mackerel.

Back to   MARSH HARBOR, it is cool and comfortable out on anchor. In the anchorage, we visited with *EVENING STAR,* Bob and Marilyn Carter, acquaintances from Cadillac, Michigan.   A fellow came alongside and asked if we knew his friend, Jack, (forgot his last name) manager of a Ben Franklin also in Cadillac.

197

Jack's nephew, Rick Nicolen is my niece's husband. A Mr. Orwell and Mr. Johnson also came over and wondered if we knew Jake Beers, president of a bank, and Dr. David Lint, an orthopedic surgeon, both well known individuals from Traverse City.

Later we did go ashore and walked the streets in hot, steamy temperatures. We purchased hand woven baskets for my friend Mary Center, Ken's sister Eunice Isaac and myself.

GREEN TURTLE BLACK SOUND May 15 – There are more fish in the sea. On our way a twenty–one inch Spanish Mackerel took my bait. Still underway, Ken filleted it on the aft deck. We had fish for supper.

We toured the village. There are many very small homes, all packed in together. Most had roosters and chickens in the yard.

MANJACK CAY – Continuing a short ways up the Atlantic side, we stop for the night at Manjack Cay, which is uninhabited. Scouting the cay in the dinghy in very shallow water, we see a few shark, a turtle, and several large fish. A sunken barge along the shore supposedly is home to many moray eels.

May 18–19 POWELL CAY – We tied to a rather rickety dock. Its deteriorated pilings were rotting off at the water line.

Between this dock and shore is a sunken sailboat, victim of a propane gas explosion and fire. Trapped inside was a 23 year old girl from the States. Rescuers were unable to reach her. They hauled the burning boat away from the dock and into shallow water. The cabin is partially out of the water at low tide. Otherwise, you see only an eerie shadow of it under the water.

Because the girl loved the area so much, her body was not removed from the boat. Her family has a memorial plaque in her name on a very large boulder on shore.

Chlorox bottles tied to sticks mark the paths to the ocean. Here you will see some of the most beautiful beaches you can possibly find. Large breakers were pounding the shore.

The weather is still favorable as we proceed north to HOG CAYS. When we arrived though, we found it lacked protection from the sea.

We went on to ALLENS-PENSACOLA. Allens-Pensacola used to be two Cays until a hurricane filled it in, joining the two.   You see remains of a missile tracking station with helicopter pad formerly used and now abandoned by the our Air Force and Navy.

The next day we scouted MORAINE CAY.   I thought the bay was churned too much for snorkeling. Still while there, Ken and Graydon put on their gear and started diving for conch. Before long, they had 20 conch in the dinghy.   After determining the cove was too exposed to weather for overnight, we returned to Allens-Pensacola.

On the beach at Allens-Pensacola, the job now is to clean the conch. This means cracking the shell, removing the conch, and throwing the innards into the water. While they were cleaning, I decided to go for a swim in the nice warm water.   Soon, however, I see a six foot shark apparently hungry and looking for a meal, being attracted by the conch innards.   Needless to say, I immediately headed for shore, and came as close to "walking on water" that a human could possibly do.

CARTER CAYS is a group of four cays and many, many rocks. Here there is an active Air Force Systems Command Missile Tracking Station.   There used to be one-hundred fifty men on hand – now there are but six.

In approaching Carter Cay, there is a range that guides you into the harbor. Even though we were almost at high tide, and following the range, we still bounced several times off the bottom.

Once inside the harbor, we dropped our anchor just off the main channel where there is a strong current. But it didn't appear safe – poor, hard holding ground. Here they suggest you swim down to make sure your anchor is dug in. These conditions were not favorable to a restful night. Plus by this time the wind was howling. We all agreed to go on to Great–Sale for a better anchorage.

Our stop at GREAT SALE was very pleasurable. A narrow foot path from our bay's anchorage led us to the ocean and past the remains of another tracking station.

Knee–deep water went out several hundred feet. The temperature of the water must have been as warm, or warmer than the air. We laid back into the shallowness, and soaked up the warmth of the water and sunshine. It was a treat.

WEST END – May 24 – Our visit to the Bahamas is nearly over as we head back across the Banks to West End. This forty five mile day was mostly in the rain – the kind where the clouds just open up and pour on you.

We reach the Jack Tar marina in early afternoon. During a brief interlude of heavy rain, we enjoyed swimming in their Olympic size pool and playing water volleyball.

Today is also Graydon and Bobbie's wedding anniversary. There is really no place to go, and it is still raining very hard. Their celebration will wait until we return to Florida.

On May 25 after a marvelous eight weeks, it is time to say "good–bye" to the Bahamas, and its beautiful white sand beaches and crystal clear water.

36

RETURN TO FLORIDA

WE LEAVE West End at 0730. We again make our calculations for the Gulf Stream current to make a landfall at North Palm Beach, Florida.

We had a nice wind on our aft quarter and clear skies for the first seven hours.

Then the rains came again. Visibility was less than 1/2 mile. It was impossible at times to see the *GRAY-BOB* a short ways ahead of us.

As we are crossing the Gulf Stream, nearing the Florida shore, we see a large freighter heading south. We wondered if we could safely cross in front of it. Ken computed our speed and distance. He decided we had a safe margin so we held our course and passed ahead of the freighter.

Almost immediately after clearing the freighter, heavy rain came down again. *GRAY-BOB* was only a short distance from us, yet we lost sight of him in the rain.

At 1635 we pulled into North Palm Beach, Florida, (nine hours and five minutes). The fellows told us we were heading for an anchorage. I began to fret because I was looking forward to being in a marina, and not on anchor again in the heavy rain. After many days on anchor, I wanted to be hooked to electric to do my hair and get dried out.

To my delight, however, our captains were "pulling my leg" and proceeded to secure alongside a dock. There we enjoyed all the facilities, including electricity.

201

Now that we were back in the States, it was necessary to report to Customs. This was done by telephone.

We went to dinner with Graydon and Bobbie to celebrate their 37th wedding anniversary. We also gave them our surplus food as we would be leaving our *PRIME TIME* with a broker to be sold. We also would be saying "good–bye", with the hope and expectation of seeing each other again in the future. *PRIME TIME* would be leaving early in the morning.

On May 26 we leave North Palm Beach at 0610. Dawn is breaking. We still need running lights as we quietly and slowly wind our way past the sleeping boaters, and the *GRAY–BOB,* and out to the ocean. By going off shore, we avoid the many bridges on the Intercoastal Waterway. We wanted to get to Fort Lauderdale before late afternoon.

The weather is still unstable – heavy rain and thunderstorms. It was not uncomfortable coming down the Atlantic Ocean except for the last hour. Along with the rain, the wind changed and seas built.

Leaving the ocean and going through the channel into Fort Lauderdale, the strong following sea made maneuvering difficult. Several power boats churned the water as they headed out to sea. We rocked from side to side.

The rain kept coming as we pulled into a slip at Pier 66.

May 27, – TIME TO GET READY TO GO HOME.
With a heavy heart we visit and settle on a broker to list *PRIME TIME* for sale. We have accomplished our goal, and Ken's dream of sailing the Mississippi, on up to Maine, and to the Bahama Islands.

Now it is time to get our "old faithful car" stored at Fort Myers. We leased a vehicle and left Fort Lauderdale at 0600. We arrived at Fort Myers in time to see friends, go to Sunday School and church, and have dinner. Then we hurried back to Fort Lauderdale to return the rental car.

The rain keeps pouring down. Several inches by now.

The next two days, in the rain, we unload *PRIME TIME* and load the car. It was surprising to find how much gear we had stowed in the boat.

PRIME TIME was moved to another slip for "showing". Feeling rather melancholy, and with mixed emotions, we drive away, knowing we were leaving a big part of us behind.

On May 29, 1984 we return to Traverse City to begin another chapter in our lives – and to our new home purchased during our visit last fall.

A NOTE OF INTEREST regarding our *PRIME TIME.*

PRIME TIME was built in Irvine, California and trucked to our dealer in Traverse City, Michigan from whom we purchased it. Our broker in Fort Lauderdale sold it to a couple from Texas. The new owners hired a captain and sailed it across the Gulf of Mexico to Texas. Upon their arrival, the wife said she wanted "no more" and the boat was again for sale. Once more *PRIME TIME* was sold. This time the owner had it trucked to his home port near San Diego, California. Thus, our *PRIME TIME* covered the perimeter of the United States and returned to her beginning.

THE END

Time to leave our PRIME TIME – Car is packed – ready to go home

APPENDIX

Useful Knots

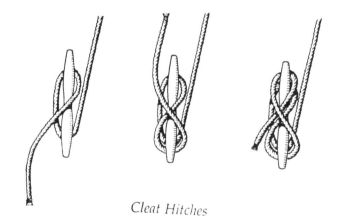

Cleat Hitches

Used *to secure a vessel*

Bowline   Rolling Hitch

The Bowline is most used and practical. It can always become untied.

Use a Rolling Hitch when tying a small line to a larger one.

reef (square) knot,

slippery reef knot

clover hitch

buntline hitch

Square knot – *Two lines tightening down. Sometimes hard to pull apart.*

Slippery reef knot – *Only a pull on the bight end loosens the knot.*

Clove hitch – *One way to secure from the bow to a piling, to the stern.*

Buntline hitch – *Its stopper knot makes it excellent for a halyard to be attached to a shackle.*

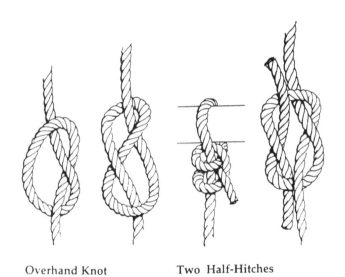

Overhand Knot   Two Half-Hitches

     Figure-eight Knot   Granny

Overhand knot and Figure Eight knot – quick and easy ways to make a stopper knot.

Two Half Hitches – An easy and safe way to secure to a railing.

A Granny – An incorrectly tied Square Knot which will work itself loose.

INDEX

Abacos 193
Adams Creek 153
Albermarle Sound 153
Allans Cay 172
Allens–Pensacola 199
America Cup Races 139
Annapolis 105 145
Apalachicola 67
Atlantic City 107
Bahama Islands 11 161
Baton Rouge 57
Beaufort, S. C. 99 153
Biscayne Channel 159
Block Island 115
Boot Key Marina 83
Boothbay Harbor, Me. 120
Brooklyn Bridge 109
Buffalo Rock 23
Buzzards Bay 115
Cairo, Ill. 36
Cape Cod Canal 115 138 140 145
Cape Girardeau 35
Cat Cay 163
Chesapeake Bay 103 145
Chic. Ship & Sanitary Canal 19 21 22 23 26
Chub Cay 163
Coinjock 153
Cos Cob, Conn. 113
CRIMSON DUKE 41
Cumberland Island 153
Current Cut 186
Customs & Immigration 161
Cuttyhunk 115
Dauphin Island 66
Daytona Beach 154

Deagles Marina 103
Delaware Canal 105
DELTA QUEEN 41
Des Plaines River 21
Destin 66
Dinner Key Marina 92 155 159
Dry Tortugas 87
Eleuthera Island 183
Ellis Island 109
Equipment 12
Everglade City 157
Experience 11
Fara Blanca Marina 155
Florida 11
Fort Myers 77
Frankfort, Mich. 16
Georgetown 180
Gloucester, Mass. 117
Govenors Island 109
Governors Harbor 185
Grand Traverse Bay 12
Great Bridge, Va. 149 151
Great Guana 197
Great Sale 200
Green Turtle Black Sound 198
Gulf of Mexico 69
Gulf Stream 161 203
Gulfport, Miss. 65
Hawks Channel 91
Hawksbill 172
Hell Gate 109 132 143
Hickman, Ky. 38
Highborn Cay 182
Hog Cays 199
Hope Town 195
Hoppies Marina 28
Hurricane Harbor 159
Hurricane Island 25
Islander Freeport 12
Jekyll Island 98

Johnson Creek 153
Kaskaskia Lock 33
Key Biscayne 93
Key West 84
Kittery Point, Me. 119
Lake Huron 12
Lake Michigan 12 15 17 26
Lake Pontchartrain 58 59
Lake Superior 12
Little Harbor 193
Little River, S. C. 153
Lockport Lock 21
Long Island Sound 109 140
LORAN C 12 15 119
Mail 25
Maine 11
Man-O-War 196
Manasquan Inlet 107 132
Marathon 155 157
Marathon 82 155 157
Marsh Harbor 194
MAYDAY 49
Memphis, Tn. 38 46 51
Merritt Island 154
Metapoisset 138
Miami 95
Milford, Conn. 113
Milwaukee, Wis. 17
Mississippi River 11 13 21 25 26 27
Missouri River 27
Morehead City 153
Mt. Katahdin 123
Nassau 167
New Bedford 139
New Orleans 51
New Providence Island 167
New Smyrna 95
New York Bay 109
Newport, R. I. 139
Norfolk, Va. 149

North Channel 12
North Manitou Island 16
North Palm Beach 203
Northport, Michigan 15
Ogden Lock 21 22
Ohio River 27
Osceola, Ark. 40
Panama City 66
Peoria Ivy Yacht Club 24
Portland, Me. 119 135
Potomac River 104
Preparation 11
Rock Sound 183
Royal Sound 188
Sandy Hook 108
Scituate, Mass. 117
Shelter Island 113
South Manitou Island 16
St. Augustine 96
St. Michaels 104
Staniel Cay 179
Staten Island 108 132
Statue of Liberty 109 132
Steamboat Channel 91
Steve's Marina 56
Stono River, S. C. 153
Thunderbolt Marina 153
Traverse City, Mich. 15 29
United States Customs 99
Useppa Island 74
Venetian Harbor 28
West Palm Beach 154
Willoughby Bay, Va. 149
Wrightsville Beach 153
Yazoo River 53

Author's note to her readers:

I hope you have enjoyed reading about our cruise which we found not only gratifying, but educational. Visiting a very small to the very large city by water gives you a different view point and challenges than by land. We also enjoyed the many anchorages, sometimes remote, where we spent numerous nights.

I hope my story encourages others, particularly women, to experience sailing for a short or an extended period of time.

My story is also intended for persons not only who have traveled by land or sea, but those merely interested in reading about other's experiences.

I wish you clear skies, fair weather, and favorable winds.

ORDER FORM

PRIME TIME PUBLISHING
5688 Balkan Court, SW
Fort Myers, Florida 33919

Please send me_____copies of:

MY HOME AFLOAT

by Dorothy Hoekwater

My payment of $9.95 per copy is enclosed. (Please add
$1.50 to cover postage, packing and handling.)

Name_____

Address_____

_____

COLOPHON

The author wrote this book using an IBM PS/1 word processor. She used her very complete journal for reference and incorporated the information onto the computer. Credit is given her husband who was of great assistance in the final editing. In addition, appreciation is given to Dave Carlson, Ralph Schultz and Victor Geha, of Lloyd Business Machines, Traverse City, for preparing camera ready copy on their Canon Laser printer.

COMPOSITION:
  IBM PS/1 computer
  CANON 811 printer

PAPER:
  Text, 60# White Offset 444 ppi
  10 PT C1S on cover

BINDING:
  Perfect bound

COVER BY:
  Remy Champt
  Traverse City, Michigan

PRINTING;
  McNaughton & Gunn, Inc.
  Saline, Michigan